# THE CLIENT MONEY ASSETS (CASS) BLUEPRINT

## For CASS 6 & 7 Firms

Asare Nicholls

*The Client Money and Assets (CASS) Blueprint:
For CASS 6 & 7 Firms*

Copyright © 2019 by Asare Nicholls

All rights reserved. This book or any portion thereof may not be reproduced or used in any manner whatsoever without the express written permission of the publisher except for the use of brief quotations in a book review.

ISBN 9781798536278

**DISCLAIMER**

This book covers UK regulatory legal issues. While care has been taken to ensure its accuracy, the author does not accept any liability for any loss, damage or other inconvenience caused as a result of any inaccuracy or errors within this book.

**DEDICATED TO**

Alexander Currie, Alan Nicholls,
Ron Digby, and Sylvester Nyamaah

"Protection of Client Assets and Money (CASS) is still a priority for the Financial Conduct Authority (FCA) and this is not going to go away... It is hugely important for market stability to ensure CASS is done right – in good times and bad."

Speech by David Lawton, Director of Markets at the FCA, delivered at the FCA CASS Conference 2014 event for CASS large firms.

# TABLE OF CONTENTS

ABOUT ASARE NICHOLLS ............................................................................ 7

INTRODUCTION ............................................................................................. 9

BACKGROUND .............................................................................................. 11

**Section 1:** GOVERNANCE ...................................................................... 23

**Section 2:** CASS REQUIREMENTS AND BEST PRACTICE ............... 47

**Section 3:** KEY PILLARS OF CASS REGULATIONS ............................ 59

**Section 4:** REPORTING REQUIREMENTS ......................................... 109

**Section 5:** The FCA ................................................................................ 123

**Section 6:** COMMON CASS FAILINGS .............................................. 127

**Section 7:** THE FUTURE OF CASS ..................................................... 131

**Section 8:** WHY CASS REGULATION WILL BECOME BLOCKCHAIN REGULATION ............................................................................................... 133

My Services .................................................................................................. 139

Bibliography ................................................................................................ 142

Index ............................................................................................................. 143

# ABOUT ASARE NICHOLLS

Asare Nicholls is a Client Money and Assets (CASS) expert who has worked in CASS for over five years. Asare previously worked in CASS supervision and CASS enforcement at the Financial Conduct Authority (FCA). Since 2015 he has worked as a specialist CASS consultant, providing CASS review, advisory and remediation services for a wide variety of firms, including Tier 1 banks, platforms, asset managers and professional services firms.

Asare was the CASS specialist on the FCA Enforcement case team that fined Towergate £2.6m and fined former Towergate Client Money Officer and CF1 (director) Timothy Philip £60,000 in addition to banning him from having direct responsibility for client money.

Whilst at the FCA, Asare also worked on the client money misappropriation cases against Darren Newton, Christine Whitehurst and Adrian Whitehurst as well as the original client money misappropriation cases against Niall O'Kelly and Lukhvir Thind.

As of 2018 these are some of only a handful CASS-related bans and fines the FCA has taken against individuals. The FCA continues to pursue a strategy of holding individuals liable for CASS failings, so this provides Asare with unique insight in advising CASS management on CASS governance.

Asare is an expert in preventing firms and senior management from receiving multi-million-pound fines from the FCA. He uses his unique insight from FCA Enforcement cases, combined with his experience as a CASS Supervisor, to help clients implement the systems and controls that are necessary to ensure compliance with the CASS rules and avoid significant fines.

As well as a CASS specialist, Asare is also a serial entrepreneur. He is the CEO and Founder of Tough Love Grad, a website that provides coaching and products to students and graduates looking to find graduate jobs. Asare is also the founder of an app publishing company.

You can connect with Asare by email at
**asare.s.nicholls@visie.co.uk**

# INTRODUCTION

Even as an ex-regulator, I can admit that the current CASS handbook is impractical, complex and unwieldy.

I have written this book to simplify your CASS understanding. This book will benefit the CF10as, Board members, senior managers, CASS staff, internal auditors and compliance staff in all firms who are involved in, or responsible for, the safe custody of assets and holding client money.

This guide attempts to streamline and collate all the required knowledge into a single source.

It creates a unified portable reference that summarises both best practice and rules. In doing so, it combines policy statements, FCA handbooks, FCA guidance, speeches and elements of the FCA business plan, as well as incorporating practical experience in the area.

**How to use this guide**

This guide is specifically designed for firms that hold client money under CASS 7 rules, and/or safe custody assets under CASS 6 rules. It is separated into headings that relate to key areas of the CASS rules. There is some overlap between sections, as many aspects of governance are relevant to multiple areas of the CASS rules.

Use this guide as an easy reference you can dip into when necessary.

## How can I help you personally?

I provide consulting, training and review services as well as digital on-call CASS support. Please do not hesitate to connect with me if you are interested in any of the above services, want to suggest improvements or just say hello.

**asare.s.nicholls@visie.co.uk**

# BACKGROUND

### What is CASS regulation?

*"A firm must arrange adequate protection for clients' assets when it is responsible for them."*
***Principle 10, FCA Sourcebook** [1]*

CASS is a set of rules and regulations that firms follow while dealing with a client's money or safe custody assets as part of a business contract. The CASS rules help to keep a client's money or assets safe if the firm fails and declares insolvency.

The objectives of CASS are to safeguard client money and assets against the risk of being used without consent (e.g. for the firm's own account) and therefore safeguard client assets against the risk of being diminished through insolvency.

This means that firms must ensure that their client's money and assets are protected and will be returned within a reasonable timeframe in the event that the firm becomes insolvent. Clients - and the FCA - must be able to be confident that the firms holding their money and assets have strong management oversight and control of their business.

CASS regulation is based on the concept of 'trust', which requires that when a client transfers money or assets to a firm, the firm segregates this money or assets and treats them separately from the firm's own money or assets. This

---

[1] https://www.fca.org.uk/about/principles-good-regulation

becomes significant when the firm then places that money or assets with a third party (i.e. a bank or custodian) as that third party needs to be aware that the money or assets is not the firm's own money or assets, but actually belongs to clients.

## Why is CASS regulation important?

FCA-regulated firms have approximately £92bn of cash and almost £11tn of assets[2] under their control. This makes them extremely important for the UK economy, but it also means that in the wake of any economic turbulence, there is an increased likelihood that some firms will become insolvent.

This makes CASS regulation extremely important to FCA regulation and to the general health of the UK financial system.

## CASS background story – How the collapse of Lehman Brothers led to the creation of the FCA's CASS supervisory unit

Client asset rule requirements have been around since the Financial Services Act of 1986, but CASS regulation became an increased FCA priority after the collapse of Lehman Brothers collapse in September 2008. The scale of this collapse brought the CASS regulation into sharp focus, as tens of billions of pounds of client money and assets were placed at risk.

When Lehman Brothers collapsed, clients ran into significant issues as they tried to reclaim their money. Client assets and money from its UK investment bank, Lehman Brothers International (Europe) (LBIE), should have been held by the

---

[2] Speech by David Lawton, Director of Markets at the FCA, delivered at the FCA CASS Conference 2014 event for CASS large firms.

firm as client money (and thus ring-fenced from the claims of the firm's general creditors). However, when clients then made claims on their funds, these claims exceeded - by a huge margin - the money that was actually being held in the segregated client money accounts.

The main problem was that LBIE operated the alternative approach to segregation of client monies (see 'Approach to segregation'):

- This meant client money was initially received into its house accounts (creating a mixed fund);

  and

- There were therefore daily reconciliations and transfers between the house and segregated accounts to ensure the correct amount was segregated.

In addition, there would have been a shortfall in the amount of client money that was in fact actually segregated, as LBIE failed to recognise some counterparties as clients. For example, it did not treat money belonging to affiliates (approximately US$3bn) as client money.

LBIE also operated a liquidity management process that swept surplus cash every night from house accounts to its US parent, including money that it should have segregated.

When LBIE was eventually placed into administration (an act known as a primary pooling event – see 'Insolvency and primary pooling events') on the morning of 15 September 2008, it could only account for approximately US$2.16 billion of money in its segregated client accounts. This amount fell far short of the client money required, by several billion dollars.

The last reconciliation before the primary pooling event was completed on the morning of 12 September, which meant that considerable sums of client money remained in LBIE's own account when the pooling took place.[3]

Complicating matters, LBIE was then pursued by unsecured creditors (non-clients) who competed for the unsegregated money (i.e. sums of client money remaining in LBIE's own account) as those funds had not been ring-fenced as they should have been. The actions of LBIE meant that much of the client money was still unsegregated – effectively rendering it up for grabs.

Four years had passed by the time the US Supreme Court deemed that the client money that should have been segregated but was not, should be ringfenced. Of course, by this time the unsegregated money had been considerably diminished by insolvency fees.

The issues highlighted by the Lehman Brothers collapse led directly to the FCA recognising the need to protect UK clients against a similar event. Consequently, the FCA developed a specialist CASS supervision unit and completed an enhancement to the CASS rules.

Since 2008, CASS has been a key regulatory focus for the FCA. It will continue to be so for the foreseeable future.

## What is client money and what are safe custody assets?

Client money and safe custody assets are the two terms that you will hear most commonly when discussing CASS regulation.

It is important that you understand exactly what they are.

---

[3] In the matter of Lehman Brothers International (Europe) (In Administration) and in the matter of the Insolvency Act 1986 [2012] UKSC 6

The definitions are below:

Client Money (investment):
*"Money a firm receives or holds for, or on behalf of, a client in the course of, or in connection with, its MiFID, stocks and shares ISA, or designated investment business which a firm treats as Client Money in accordance with the Client Money rules."*
FCA handbook

Safe Custody Assets:
*"A designated investment or asset, other than property, held for or on behalf of a client for which the firm is accountable which a firm treats as safe custody assets in accordance with the custody rules."*

Put simply, client money is the money a firm holds on your behalf for investment purposes.

Safe custody assets are assets (not property) that a firm holds on your behalf.

## Where do the CASS rules come from?

CASS rules come from the Client Assets Sourcebook, which forms part of the FCA Handbook. There are six types of 'rules', set out below.

Note that the bracketed capital letters have been added for your easy reference - they are not denoted this way in the FCA handbook.

1. **Rules (R):** These are binding and if breached can lead to disciplinary action. It should be noted that the FCA's principles for business (see below) are given the status of rules.

2. **Directions (D):** These dictate the content required for applications for authorisation by the FCA.
3. Statements of principle for approved persons (P): These are binding on approved persons such as the CF10a or SMF in charge of CASS.
4. **Evidential provision (E):** A rule that is not binding in its own right, but which would provide indicative evidence of compliance with another rule.
5. **Behaviour** that does not amount to market abuse **(B):** Behaviour that does not amount to market abuse.
6. **Guidance (G):** This is either an explanation of other rules or a recommendation. These are not binding and therefore failure to follow guidance cannot lead to disciplinary action. However, it should be noted that failure to follow guidance can sometimes be interpreted as a breach of a principle.

At the time of writing, the sourcebook is made up of 12 chapters as well as one transitional provision and six schedules. The chapters and schedules are:

- CASS 1 Application and general provisions
- CASS 1A CASS firm classification and operational oversight
- CASS 3 Collateral
- CASS 5 Client money: insurance distribution activity
- CASS 6 Custody rules
- CASS 7 Client money rules
- CASS 7A Client money distribution and transfer
- CASS 8 Mandates
- CASS 9 Information to clients

- CASS 10 CASS resolution pack
- CASS 11 Debt management client money chapter
- CASS 12 Commodity Futures Trading Commission Part 30 exemption order
- CASS TP 1 Transitional Provisions
- CASS Sch 1 Record keeping requirements
- CASS Sch 2 Notification requirements
- CASS Sch 3 Fees and other required payments
- CASS Sch 4 Powers exercised
- CASS Sch 5 Rights of actions for damages
- CASS Sch 6 Rules that can be waived

It should be noted that the CASS rules are subject to change and are often updated.

## Other relevant rules

Principles for Business:
The FCA Handbook contains 11 key Principles for Business which FCA regulated firms must follow. If a firm breaches any of the principles it is liable to disciplinary action.

The 11 key principles are:

1. **Integrity** - A firm must conduct its business with integrity.
2. **Skill, care and diligence** - A firm must conduct its business with due skill, care and diligence.
3. **Management and control** - A firm must take reasonable care to organise and control its affairs responsibly and effectively, with adequate risk management systems.
4. **Financial prudence** - A firm must maintain adequate financial resources.

5. **Market conduct** - A firm must observe proper standards of market conduct.
6. **Customers' interests** - A firm must pay due regard to the interests of its customers and treat them fairly.
7. **Communications with clients** - A firm must pay due regard to the information needs of its clients and communicate information to them in a way which is clear, fair and not misleading.
8. **Conflicts of interest** - A firm must manage conflicts of interest fairly, both between itself and its customers and between a customer and another client.
9. **Customers: relationships of trust** - A firm must take reasonable care to ensure the suitability of its advice and discretionary decisions for any customer who is entitled to rely upon its judgement.
10. **Clients' assets** - A firm must arrange adequate protection for clients' assets when it is responsible for them.
11. **Relations with regulators** - A firm must deal with its regulators in an open and co-operative way and must disclose to the FCA anything relating to the firm of which the FCA would reasonably expect notice.[4]

The most relevant key principles for CASS firms are:

- Principle 2 (Skill, care and diligence)
- Principle 3 (Management and control)
- Principle 6 (Customers' interests)
- Principle 10 (Clients' assets)
- Principle 11 (Relations with regulators).
- These principles are often cited in CASS enforcement cases.

---

4 https://handbook.fca.org.uk/handbook/PRIN/2/1.html?date=2016-10-03

## SYSC:
The Senior Management Arrangements, Systems and Controls (SYSC) sourcebook contained within the FCA Handbook requires firms to establish and maintain systems and controls appropriate to their business and the specific risks associated with their business.

## COBS:
The Conduct of Business Sourcebook (COBS) contained within the FCA Handbook contains rules and guidance relating to the relationship between firms and its customers. These rules require the firm to act honestly and fairly in the best interests of its customers.

## MiFID:
The Markets in Financial Instruments Directive (MiFID) is European Union legislation that provides regulation for investment services. MiFID rules were transposed into the CASS sourcebook and it therefore provides more detail around rules such as safeguarding assets (Article 16), depositing client assets (Article 17), depositing client funds (Article 18) and use of financial instruments (Article 19).

## FSMA and RAO:
The Financial Services and Markets Act (FSMA) states that no person can carry on a regulated activity unless they are authorised to do so. The Regulated Activity Order (RAO) sets out holding or safeguarding client assets as a regulated activity. It is therefore a criminal offence to hold and/or safeguard client assets without the required authorisation.

## Trust Law:
English trust law concerns the creation and protection of asset funds, which are usually held by one party for another's

benefit.[5] Therefore, when a client transfers money or assets to a firm to hold on their behalf, these assets are governed by trust law and subject to a legal agreement between the firm and the client.

With regards to client money, trust is established via the client agreement, which must acknowledge trust and segregation. The statutory trust status of client money is further protected via the acknowledgement letter (see the section on A Acknowledgement letters). Without an acknowledgement letter, there is a risk that a third party would not segregate client money in the event of a default.

## Significant CASS fines

One of the key enforcement tools used by the FCA are fines. Since 2008 there have been a number of relevant and high-profile enforcement actions against firms for CASS failures.

Some of the most relevant cases include:

### JP Morgan 2010

- Fined £33m for failing to segregate client money held by its futures and options business.

### BNY Mellon (BNYM) 2015

- Fined £126m for failing to adequately safeguard client assets. Amongst other failings:
- BNYM failed to conduct external reconciliations.
- BNYM failed to make some custody assets separately identifiable from proprietary assets.

---

[5] JE Martin, *Hanbury & Martin: Modern Equity* (19th edn Sweet & Maxwell 2012) ch 2, 49

- BNYM failed to create CASS-specific governance arrangements.
- BNYM failed to provide CASS-specific training.

### **Towergate Underwriting Group 2016**

- Fined £2.6m.
- Towergate's Client Money Officer was fined £60k.
- Towergate made withdrawals of money from Towergate's client money bank accounts without properly considering the implications of these transfers. This resulted in accumulated deficits of £5 million in the client money bank accounts.

### **Aviva Pension Trustees 2016**

- Fined £8.2m for oversight failures of CASS outsourcing arrangements.
- The FCA made it clear that other firms with similar outsourcing arrangements should take this as a warning that there is no excuse for not having robust controls and oversight systems in place.

Having had experience of working on CASS enforcement cases, in my opinion it should be noted that no firm or individual deliberately weakens client asset protection.

However, the best intentions aren't always a protection against CASS failings and fines. To avoid fines it is important that strong systems and controls are put in place along with regular reviews.

# SECTION 1:

# GOVERNANCE

## Governance definition

Good CASS governance is the bedrock of successful CASS compliance. In order to consider the importance of good CASS governance, we must first define the word 'governance'.

The Cambridge Dictionary defines it as *"the way that organisations or countries are managed at the highest level, and the systems for doing this"*.

It is important that good CASS governance is cascaded from the highest level of the organisation, and that good management and systems are put in place.

## Governance aims

The objectives of CASS governance are to:

- Reduce CASS risk for the firm and clients.
- Provide evidence of processes and controls.
- Spread the regulatory burden across all relevant areas.
- Achieve CASS compliance as cost effectively as possible.

Knowing these objectives leaves us with the question: what does 'Good CASS Governance' look like?

Well, two key components are: having a complete picture of CASS risks; and having a detailed understanding of what to do to manage those risks, i.e. controls.

A CASS management team should ensure that CASS controls exist, are adequate and are working. A key part of that is creating an appropriate reporting structure and Management Information (MI).

## CASS governance: best practice

Best practice for a CASS governance structure is:

- A competent CF10a or senior manager with responsibility for CASS operational oversight, having experience in CASS regulation and operations
- The CF10a or senior manager with responsibility for CASS operational oversight should sit on a CASS Forum or Committee; with input from the CASS team, Compliance, Finance, IT, Risk, Audit, Operations, and Legal as appropriate.
- The agenda at the CASS Forum or Committee should include breaches and issues, supplier reporting, the CASS resolution pack, the Client Money and Assets Return (CMAR), the operational model, policy, procedures, training and MI.
- The CF10a or senior manager with responsibility for CASS operational oversight should escalate important issues from the CASS Committee to the Board.
- Key decisions should be recorded in the minutes of the CASS Forum or Committee.
- The CF10a or senior manager with responsibility for CASS operational oversight should make sure the minutes of the governance meetings are comprehensive, up to date and available.

## Key CASS documentation

Another key aspect of CASS governance is having the correct documentation in place.

The below documents are considered best practice for CASS firms to have available:

SECTION 1:

- CASS framework aka the CASS policy document
- Procedure documents for key CASS processes
- CASS Management Information
- CASS rules map
- CASS breach log
- Accountability matrix
- CASS Resolution Pack
- Training records
- Board minutes where CASS issues have been escalated or CASS updates have been provided
- Client agreements
- Daily CASS checklist
- CASS reconciliation sign-off pack

## What is CASS rule mapping?

Firms are required to conduct an ongoing CASS rule-mapping exercise. In this exercise, the firm assess all CASS rules and maps them to the firm's relevant processes and procedures.

Where gaps exist, a firm should seek to implement processes to fill those gaps. Where processes and procedures only partially meet the rules, a firm should assess the remediation action that is required.

As part of the rule-mapping process, the firm should assess inherent risk, control efficiency and residual risk for each rule. The firm should also produce a CASS footprint and money flow diagrams.

It is important that CASS rule-mapping is an ongoing process and that there is a defined process in place to identify both process changes and rule changes.

## CASS footprint diagram

A CASS footprint diagram is a diagram that identifies the flow of money and assets and highlights CASS risks within these flows. As part of a CASS footprint diagram a firm should always consider legacy products and suspense accounts.

## CASS framework document - aka the CASS policy

Each firm should have a CASS framework document (aka the CASS policy)
that fully documents the governance structure of the firm, including committee reporting lines, escalation process and so on.

In addition, the document should:

- Detail the firm's permissions.
- Define roles and responsibilities for key CASS personnel including the CF10a or senior manager with responsibility for CASS operational oversight.
- Define the firm's CASS type i.e. small, medium or large. Sets out the roles and responsibilities for the three lines of defence.
- Set out the roles and responsibilities for the three lines of defence.
- Detail the firm's rules mapping policy.
- Detail the firm's due diligence requirements and policy.
- Define the firm's breach reporting policy.
- Set out the firm's CASS resolution pack policy.
- Detail any CMAR assumptions and policies.

- Define CASS Management Information requirements.
- Define recordkeeping requirements.
- Define client on boarding policy.
- Set CASS standards around CASS 6 & 7, specifically detailing the type and frequency of reconciliations, treatment of discrepancies and shortfalls.
- Detail the diversification policy.
- Define the bank and custodian selection criteria.

## CASS procedures

Firms should have a comprehensive set of CASS procedures. These should be identified in the rule-mapping exercise.

## CASS Management Information (MI)

CASS MI is a key tool for evidencing the effective oversight of CASS. CF10a or senior managers with responsibility for CASS operational oversights should ensure that the firm has effective CASS MI that identifies and reports on key indicators such as breaches, CASS holdings, unresolved reconciliation breaks, and picks up any key trends.

When analysing breaches, it is important to ensure that the root cause of any breach is also considered. This helps to ensure that any systematic issues are identified.

In addition, CASS MI should:

- Be produced monthly by the business, for review at the CASS Forum/Committee and by the firm's governing board.
- Include data for previous reporting month and ideally

take a rolling 12-month approach.
- Include any concerns raised in compliance reviews or internal audits that are tracked through to conclusion.
- Include CASS training status of key personnel i.e. last trained and next due.

## Breach analysis and breach log

A key part of CASS MI is CASS breach analysis. Good CASS breach analysis should include:

Breach reporting, root cause analysis, area breakdown, breach by rule type.
A strong and documented approach to breach escalation and incident management, including the considerations that should be made when ascertaining whether breaches require immediate FCA notification or not.
A clear program of activities planned to remediate ongoing issues.

In addition, it is important to maintain a CASS breach log. Firms should ensure that the breach log is up to date, current and complete. The breach log should include the date, breach cause, breach description, relevant rule, remediation actions and identification of whether the breach will be reported to the FCA.

## Daily CASS checklist and CASS calendar

A CASS calendar is one of the key controls a CF10a or senior manager with responsibility for CASS operational oversight should consider for themselves and their team. This should include daily, weekly, monthly and yearly tasks and should be retained as evidence for audits and FCA visits.

Another key control is a CASS checklist. This should record key tasks and dates, including:

- Due dates for regulatory submissions e.g. size of firm, CMAR etc
- Key dates for record-keeping updates
- Due diligence renewal dates
- Training dates
- Yearly "basis of reconciliations" assessment
- Review of Banking Exemption (if applicable)
- Reconciliation control sheet daily reminder
- Policies and procedures review date
- The date of the board update from the CF10a or senior manager with responsibility for CASS operational oversight

## Three lines of defence

To ensure the effectiveness of an organisation's CASS governance framework, the board and senior management need to be able to rely on adequate line functions – including monitoring and assurance functions – within the organisation.

The 'Three lines of defence' model is a way of explaining the relationship between these functions as well as a guide to the way that responsibilities should be divided:

1. First line of defence: Business line ownership

    a. The Operations Department – should have policies and procedures in place to adhere to CASS rules
    
    b. The Operational Risk Department – should complete risk assessments on CASS risks

2. <u>Second line of defence:</u> Compliance and CASS team

   a. The CASS team should be responsible for oversight of the firm's operational compliance with CASS, and for reporting to the firm's governing body in respect of that oversight.

   b. The compliance team should provide effective oversight, advisory, monitoring and reporting arrangements. Compliance should be responsible for the Compliance monitoring plan and breach reporting. As part of Compliance's monitoring responsibilities, it should assess the adequacy and effectiveness of the procedures put in place to comply with CASS.

3. <u>Third line of defence:</u> Internal Audit

   a. Internal audit should provide additional independent review.

## Three lines of defence: best practice

Best practice for Risk, Compliance and Internal Audit teams entails:

- A clear split between monitoring and advice (independent and objective)
- An assessment of materiality of CASS risks and breaches. Literally step-by-step, nothing is left out
- Each review should begin with an assessment of risks which the review is the based on i.e. reviewing the highest risk areas
- Timely follow-up of any issues identified by reviews
- Compliance should have CASS technical knowledge and expertise in order to be able to conduct robust and independent CASS reviews

- The Internal Audit function should have clear responsibilities with regards to CASS and conduct periodic independent CASS related reviews over the firm's CASS arrangements
- CASS reviews should form part of the Internal Audit annual review plans.
- Internal Audit annual review plans should be structured on a risk basis and should be reviewed on a periodic basis to capture new issues or risks.
- Members of the Internal Audit function should have enough CASS knowledge to be able to conduct robust and independent CASS reviews.

## How to determine the CASS review responsibilities of second and third line

One of the biggest causes of confusion regarding the CASS three lines of defence model is the relative responsibilities of Compliance and Internal Audit with regards to CASS reviews.

It is expected that Compliance and Internal Audit have clear and defined responsibilities with regards to CASS assurance. This confusion is further compounded by the fact there is a yearly external audit review of CASS and there can often be a feeling that work is being repeated.

The first thing to establish when designing your CASS three lines of defence structure is that trying to avoid duplication with external audit should not factor into the design of the three lines of defence.

This is because the FCA expects firms to complete internal and independent assurance on CASS controls, separate from the external audit process. It is expected that control failings are identified internally, and any control failings that are identified externally are likely to increase the severity of FCA action.

Please consider quotes from the FCA in relation to two relevant CASS fines:

1. From the Final Notice against Aviva Pension Trustees UK Limited[1]:

> *"The Authority considers the Firms' failings to be serious for the following reasons:*
> *[...](3) some of the Firms' failings were drawn to the Firms' attention by the Firms' external CASS auditors, the Authority and the Skilled Person, rather than through their own compliance monitoring. During the Relevant Period, the Firms' internal audit reviews were infrequent and oversight of the outsourced CASS functions was inadequate."*

2. From the Final Notice against Towergate Underwriting Group Limited[2]:

> *"TUGL also relied on its external auditors as a key control despite the fact that in January 2010 the Authority had raised an industry wide concern on firms' overreliance on CASS audit reports rather than performing their own assurance checks."*

It is clear that the FCA fully expects firms to perform their own assurance checks, separate to that of the external audit.

---

[1] https://www.fca.org.uk/publication/final-notices/aviva-pension-trustees-uk-limited-aviva-wrap-uk-limited.pdf

[2] https://www.fca.org.uk/publication/final-notices/towergate-underwriting-group-limited.pdf

SECTION 1:

Now that we have established that duplication of the work of external auditors should not be a consideration, we are still left with the relative CASS review responsibilities of Compliance Monitoring and Internal Audit.

It is wise to take one of two approaches:

**1.** Divide the CASS rulebook into key areas (see my own suggested CASS universe structure below) and rate each area in terms of risk on a periodic basis. Divide review responsibilities for each area between Internal Audit and Compliance Monitoring, and ensure each area within the CASS rules is reviewed within an agreed time period. Internal Audit will usually have the responsibility of reviewing Compliance Monitoring's coverage of CASS as part of its responsibilities.

**2.** Give Compliance Monitoring the responsibility of reviewing compliance risk and Internal Audit the responsibility of reviewing process risk. What I mean by that is that Compliance Monitoring would review whether the CASS rules are being followed correctly, with the correct processes in place, and Internal Audit would ensure that there are adequate controls around those processes. CASS expertise is still required for both areas but there would be a clear division of responsibility.

## Suggested CASS universe for internal audit and compliance monitoring reviews

It is my suggestion that rather than doing a "full CASS review", as many firms attempt to do each year, it is more prudent to divide the CASS rulebook into key areas and review each area on a periodic basis.

The reason I believe that it is better to review one or two CASS areas at a time is because CASS is too large and complex to be reviewed in the normal review period of a month. To properly complete a full CASS review would take several months.

The issue is that firms tend to try shoehorning a CASS review into their own timeframes, rather than the other way around. This is understandable, but if only a month or two can be dedicated to a CASS review, it is better to select one or two areas so that some value can be gained with a deep dive.

In terms of how to divide the CASS rulebook, please see my own suggested CASS universe structure below:

**1.** CASS Governance Framework (medium size topic)
   1.1 CASS Oversight Forum – attendance, agenda, MI and decision making
   1.2 Completeness of policies, processes and framework documents
   1.3 CASS checklists – daily, weekly and annual checklists
   1.4 Board reporting and escalation
   1.5 Breaches – materiality assessment, root cause and timeliness of reporting
   1.6 CASS rule-mapping – update procedure
   1.7 CASS training – tailored training for different staff, population trained and frequency
   1.8 Second line of defence – frequency and completeness of monitoring

**2.** Record Keeping (small sized topic)
   2.1 Document management – retaining records for required periods
   2.2 Diversification
   2.3 Acknowledgement letters and custody agreements

- update procedure and template adherence
    - 2.4 Due diligence – completion procedure, recording outcomes and adherence to FCA guidance
    - 2.5 Prudent segregation
3. Client Money and Assets Return (CMAR) (small sized topic)
    - 3.1 Completeness and accuracy
    - 3.2 Timeliness of submission
4. CASS Resolution Pack (medium sized topic)
    - 4.1 Access for insolvency practitioner
    - 4.2 Link testing
    - 4.3 Availability of documentation within required timeframes
    - 4.4 Update procedure
5. Reconciliations (large sized topic)
    - 5.1 Methodology
    - 5.2 Frequency
    - 5.3 Completeness and accuracy
    - 5.4 Break investigation and funding decision
    - 5.5 Top ups and withdrawals following reconciliation
    - 5.6 Aging of breaks and unallocated/unidentified aging
6. Delivery Versus Payment Exemption (medium sized topic)
    - 6.1 Controls around the 1/3 day exemption period
7. Mandates (small sized topic)
    - 7.1 Completeness
    - 7.2 Instruction versus performance
8. Payments, Income and Settlements (large sized topic)

8.1 Bank transfers in and out

8.2 Cheque receipts and payments

8.3 Interest

8.4 Physical assets and receipts

8.5 Fees

8.6 Corporate actions

8.7 Cleared funds

8.8 Overpayments

**9.** Client Categorisation (small sized topic)

9.1 Onboarding controls for categorisation and subsequent CASS treatment

## CASS training

*Clever Neily.*

Knowledgeable staff are key to ensuring a firm meets its CASS requirements and remains compliant. Trained staff will prevent breaches and identify systemic failures in procedures. Training programs should therefore be designed and delivered to all staff with CASS touch points.

Best practice entails:

- Different levels of annual training throughout the firm. i.e. in-depth training for CF10a and senior CASS managers, with specific reconciliation training for reconciliation staff
- Tests to measure the effectiveness of training/key learning objectives
- Training records available for inspection to provide evidence for completion of the program as well as continuous learning
- CASS calendar records future training schedule

SECTION 1:

- An annual review of training requirements
- Ensuring key staff can speak knowledgeably about the rules that impact them
- Annual awareness sessions for Board and senior management members

## Outsourcing models

There are two types of outsourcing models within CASS – literally the 'Model A arrangement' and the 'Model B arrangement'.

Whether a firm retains regulatory responsibility depends on which model arrangement it enters into.

Model A arrangement
This exists where an outsourced provider, known as the third party administrator (TPA), simply agrees to provide specific services to the firm. In this arrangement, the firm retains full regulatory responsibility for CASS. An example is if a firm chooses to outsource the performance of CASS reconciliations without changing its client agreements.

Model B arrangement
This exists where a firm and a Third Party Administrator (TPA) agree that the TPA will take full responsibility for compliance with some or all of the requirements within CASS. In this arrangement, the TPA would need authorisation to hold or control client money or custody assets, and the firm's clients would have to *also* enter into an agreement with the TPA which states that the TPA will be responsible to the client for CASS protection.

This is usually done in the form of a tripartite agreement between the firm, the TPA and the client. Due to the fact the clients enters into a separate agreement with the TPA, it is not technically an outsourcing agreement - but is often referred to as such. Please note that whenever I refer to outsourcing I am referring to the Model A arrangement.

## Outsourcing oversight

SYSC 8.1.6 states that – *"If a firm outsources critical or important operational functions or any relevant services and activities, it remains fully responsible for discharging all of its obligations under the regulatory system."*[3]

In short, this means that under a Model A arrangement, the FCA will still hold you, and not your outsourcing provider, accountable for your outsourced functions. You cannot outsource your CASS control risks and issues.

The oversight of the firm's CASS outsource provider needs to be detailed, and KPIs should state more than 'compliance with CASS regulations'.

The oversight requires:

- Due diligence prior to engagement, to ensure that the outsourcing provider has sufficient CASS capabilities.
- Terms, KPIs and MI that ensure appropriate pressure can be applied to correct underperformance.
- Ongoing oversight of the outsourcing provider i.e. receiving, reading and actively reviewing the outputs from the outsourcing provider.

As part of your oversight, the FCA would expect evidence of the above as well as:

---

[3] https://www.handbook.fca.org.uk/handbook/SYSC/8/1.html

- Visits from the CF10a or senior manager with responsibility for CASS operational oversight to the outsource provider, and regular meetings between the two parties coupled with minutes of those meetings.
- Monthly MI from the outsourcing provider, measured against associated KPIs.

One of the most common issues with oversight of CASS outsourced functions is a lack of focus on specific CASS issues. Due diligence of CASS outsource providers should focus on CASS oversight capabilities.

Factors to be considered:
- Breach reporting and resolution
- What CASS MI will be produced.

## Outsourcing KPIs

Penalties within the outsourcing agreement should be linked to key MI such as:
- Unresolved reconciliation discrepancy ageing
- Percentage of breaches caused by outsourced provider failures
- Percentage of outsourced tasks completed
- Speed of breach reporting after discovery.

## Breaches

When a firm has failed to follow Principle 10 or a specific CASS rule, this is known as a CASS breach.
Firms should establish guidelines and criteria that can be assessed when considering whether a breach is sufficiently material to warrant reporting to FCA.

The firm should record the:

- Cause of the breach
- Materiality of the breach i.e. how significant it is
- Length of breach
- Remedial action undertaken.

CASS breaches should be notified to the FCA depending on their significance and materiality. A firm should notify the FCA without delay if:

- It is unable to distinguish client money held for one client, from client money held for any other client, and/or from its own money.
- It has inaccurate CASS records or can no longer maintain accurate CASS records.
- It is, or will be, unable to perform its CASS reconciliations.
- If having carried out a reconciliation it has not, or is unable, in any material respect, to pay a shortfall into a client bank account or withdraw an excess by the close of business on the day that the reconciliation is performed.[4]

Reporting breaches to the FCA should be clear, concise and describe the remedial action being taken.

---

[4] https://www.handbook.fca.org.uk/handbook/CASS/Sch/2.pdf

## Audit Reports

All regulated investment firms must send the FCA an annual CASS assurance report. This is completed by an external auditor, however, it is the responsibility of the CF10a or the senior manager with responsibility for CASS operational oversight to:

- Understand the findings in audit reports
- Oversee follow-up actions
- Log and report breaches if necessary.

## FCA Visits

Firm visits are a key part of the FCA's supervisory toolkit. The FCA will usually want to have meetings about key CASS risks during a CASS supervisory visit.

A CF10a or the senior manager with responsibility for CASS operational oversight has a personal responsibility during an FCA CASS visit to:

- Ensure that staff within the organization, including the most senior people, are aware of the visit and that their attendance may be required
- Understand the scope of the business
- Be able to explain the firm's CASS governance structure
- Understand the firm's CMAR and information that contributes to it
- Understand and explain what CASS controls are in place
- Understand and explain plans for CASS compliance in the coming year
- Understand the firm's CASS breaches and remediation

actions
- Be aware of any outsourcing arrangements that the firm has in place and explain the oversight of these
- Demonstrate how the firm is comfortable that it is complying with CASS
- Explain how they train their staff and how they ensure that CASS knowledge is spread throughout the firm.

When organising meetings for an FCA visit, a firm should ensure that they invite the correct people with relevant experience, who fully understand the process that they are responsible for.

Best practice for an FCA visit includes providing all the affected staff with interview preparation, so that they can practice being asked about their roles, responsibilities and the CASS rules that impact them.

Staff who are asked to attend the meetings should understand the breaches in their area and must be able to explain any remediation action that the firm put in place.

When preparing for close-out meetings with the FCA, a firm should:

- Ensure the correct people attend and that senior management make themselves available.
- Ensure that any misunderstandings are clarified before the FCA leave. Do not be afraid to challenge the FCA's interpretation as misunderstandings can appear in the FCA report as remediation points.
- Make notes of the issues discussed

## Post-visit follow-up

SECTION 1:

The FCA will usually send a follow-up letter within eight weeks of their visit.
This letter usually includes remediation points with target completion dates.
Following the receipt of the letter and remediation points, a firm should regularly update the FCA on their remediation progress.

Any issue which will impact the timeline should be shared immediately. The firm should ensure that all parts of the issue have been considered and remediated before claiming to have resolved the issue.

## Governance comfort level checklist

Below is a mental checklist that you can use to ensure comfort that your CASS governance is meeting best practice. Work through these steps and address any deficiencies as a priority.

- √ The firm has a reliable and complete inventory of current and legacy products and related components (e.g. accounts, safe custody arrangements).
- √ All associated documentation is readily to hand, complete and accurate.
- √ All staff are sufficiently trained to understand the rules in order to perform competent calculations and reconciliations.
- √ The firm's approach to CASS reconciliations is in accordance with industry best practice.
- √ All the CASS touch points within the transactional workflow have been mapped and documented.
- √ Client asset compliance is properly considered whenever

processes and systems are built or changed.

√ Segregation is always timely and accurate.

√ Reconciliations can be relied upon to identify and make good any individual client shortfalls.

√ CASS funding transfers are always made by close of business.

√ CASS records and management information can always be relied upon.

√ Strong controls are maintained over all CASS processes.

# SECTION 2:
# CASS REQUIREMENTS AND BEST PRACTICE

SECTION 2: CASS REQUIREMENTS AND BEST PRACTICE

## Introduction

Whenever you hold or control client money or safe custody assets as part of your business, you must follow the rules that are set out in the Client Assets Sourcebook (CASS). The FCA require firms to implement appropriate processes and controls for each CASS rule.

While this appears simple in practice, a lot of firms fall short due to the sheer number of rules in place. With CASS rules, the devil is often in the detail, and firms frequently concentrate on a small group of rules that they are aware of, which leaves them exposed to the risk of a serious breach of the CASS rules elsewhere.

What follows is a comprehensive summary of the key CASS rules. Use this to help protect your firm from an inadvertent breach.

## CASS permissions

A firm should ensure it has one of these permissions in place if it is to be responsible for client money or custody assets in the course of business.

There are three types of CASS permissions relating to investment businesses:

- Permission to hold Client Money[1]: allows a firm to hold and/or control client money on behalf of customers.
- Arranging safeguarding and administration of assets permission[2]: solely allows a firm to arrange for one or

---

1 https://www.handbook.fca.org.uk/handbook/PERG/2/
2 https://www.handbook.fca.org.uk/handbook/PERG/2/Annex2.html

more other firms to safeguard and administer custody assets.
- Safeguarding and administration of assets (without arranging) permission[3]: allows a firm to hold and/or control custody assets.

Permissions are granted by the Authorisations Department at the FCA and are applied for via an online application form.

## European Economic Area (EEA) firm passporting and non-EEA firm branch rules

Under The Markets in Financial Instruments Directive (MiFID), EEA registered firms, that are registered outside the UK, are permitted to carry on regulated activities in the UK without having to be fully authorised.

This is known as 'passporting'. It exempts EEA firms from having to comply with CASS as these firms will comply with the MiFID obligations in their home state.

All UK registered firms are still required to comply with CASS regardless of the status of any EEA registered parent firm.

Non-EEA registered firms operating via a UK branch are still required to comply with CASS in the same way as if they were registered in the UK.

## CASS exemptions

There are two key exemptions to the CASS rules:

---

[3] https://www.handbook.fca.org.uk/handbook/PERG/2/Annex2.html

## SECTION 2: CASS REQUIREMENTS AND BEST PRACTICE

1. Banking exemption[4]

    a. This exemption allows firms with permission to accept deposits (banks) to hold money as a deposit. Money held as a deposit will normally be held in the firm's own name and form part of the firm's assets and therefore, if the firm fails, the assets are not ring-fenced from the firm's general assets.

2. Delivery versus payment (DVP) exemption

    a. Both the custody rules (CASS 6) and client money rules (CASS 7) currently allow firms to disapply the rules during the course of a 'delivery versus payment' transaction through a commercial settlement system if certain conditions are met.[5]

    b. The rules also permit managers of regulated collective investment schemes (CIS) to make use of the DVP window for the purpose of settling a transaction, in relation to units in a regulated collective investment scheme – meaning that settlement amounts are not protected by CASS rules during this window.[6]

Other exemptions include the temporary handling of custody assets. This occurs when a firm is handling a client's custody assets on temporary basis, normally no longer than one business day[7]. However, despite the fact that the firm is exempt when handling custody assets it is still expected to comply with Principle 10.

---

4 CASS 7.10.16
5 CASS 6.1.12 and CASS CASS 7.11.14- CASS 7.11.29
6 CASS 7.11.21
7 CASS 6.1.15

## Banking exemption

If a firm takes advantage of the banking exemption and has circumstances in which money would cease to be treated within the banking exemption, this needs to be stated in the client's terms of business agreement.[8]

In any case, firms are required to state in the client's terms of business agreement that they are using the banking exemption.[9]

If a firm chooses to use the banking exemption for some of its business and it also holds client money as a trustee, in accordance with the client money rules in relation to other business for that client, the firm will be required to make both statements to the relevant clients within the client's terms of business agreement.

Firms should ensure that they have assessed their own activities to determine whether they do fall outside the banking exemption.

Where a firm using the banking exemption receives money which, but for the exemption, would otherwise be held as client money, the firm is expected to allocate these receipts of money promptly and no later than 10 business days following receipt. However, failing to allocate the money to clients promptly does not affect the status of how the money is held.[10]

---

**8** CASS 7.10.20

**9** CASS 7.10.19

**10** CASS 7.10.21

# SECTION 2: CASS REQUIREMENTS AND BEST PRACTICE

## Delivery Versus Payment exemption (DVP) commercial settlement

Firms using commercial settlement systems are allowed a 'three-day window' during which the DVP exclusion may apply[11], however each client's agreement must be obtained when holding its assets or monies within the DVP window.[12]

When a client makes a purchase, the DVP window starts from the date of the client's payment and then closes at the earlier of:

- The date the relevant DVP transaction settles; or
- The close of business on the third business day following the date the client fulfils its payment obligation to the firm. [13]

Where delivery of the asset to the client has not occurred by the close of business on the third business day, the firm will need to treat the money as client money until such time as the delivery by the firm to the client does occur. [14]

The firm will need to ensure it incorporates this money into its internal and external client money reconciliations and keeps appropriate records of such transactions.

When a client makes a sale, the DVP window starts from the date the client fulfils its delivery obligation to the firm and then closes at the earlier of:

---

[11] CASS 7.11.14
[12] CASS 7.11.20
[13] CASS 7.11.14
[14] CASS 7.11.14

*This will be key if whole of market rolled out

- The date the relevant DVP transaction settles; or
- The third business day following the date the client fulfils its delivery obligation to the firm. [15]

Where payment to the client hasn't occurred by the close of business on the third business day because the transaction has not yet settled, the firm will need to treat the asset as a custody asset until such time as payment by the firm to the client occurs.[16]

Until a DVP transaction in respect of a client's sale settles, a firm may, if its regulatory permissions allow, segregate its own money as client money, at an amount equivalent to the value at which that client's custody asset is reasonably expected to settle. [17]

Firms using commercial settlement systems need to have controls in place that check that settlement timescales fall within those that are prescribed.

Firms need to ensure they have procedures for:

- Identifying transactions which fall outside the window and protecting these amounts; and
- Promptly segregating amounts that settle before the window closes.
- Firms need to ensure that agreements with clients include the client's agreement to the use of the DVP window[18] – this may require amendment to their existing

---

[15] CASS 6.1.12
[16] CASS 6.1.12
[17] CASS 6.1.12
[18] CASS 6.1.12E

terms of business agreements and/or a repapering exercise with their customer base.

## Delivery Versus Payment exemption (DVP) for regulated Collective Investment Schemes (CIS) For Authorised Fund Managers (AFM)

Authorised Fund Managers (AFM) are allowed a 'one-day window' during which the DVP exclusion may apply. However, AFMs will not be required to protect the value of redemption proceeds as client money before they have received that money. [19]

At times a firm may receive money that would otherwise be client money, from a client, in relation to the issue of units in a regulated collective investment scheme. If this money has not been passed on to the trustee/depository by the close of business on the business day following receipt, the AFM must segregate it and treat it in accordance with the client money rules.

Equally, at times a firm may also receive money that would otherwise be client money, in the course of redeeming units in a regulated collective investment scheme. If this has not been passed on to the unit holder/client by the close of business on the business day following receipt, the AFM must segregate it and treat it in accordance with the client money rules. [20]

## Client categorisation

There are three types of client that a firm will deal with:

---

[19] CASS 7.11.21
[20] CASS 7.11.21

1. Retail clients: an individual who is neither a professional client nor an eligible counterparty.
2. Professional clients, who may be either:
   - An individual for whom the firm undertakes an adequate assessment of the expertise, experience and knowledge of the client that gives reasonable assurance, in light of the nature of the transactions or services envisaged, that the client is capable of making his own investment decisions and understanding the risks involved.
   - A per se professional client.

     Each of the following is considered a per se professional client unless it is considered an eligible counterparty: an investment firm; a credit institution; an insurance company; a collective investment scheme authorised under the UCITS Directive or its management company; a pension fund or its management company; another regulated financial institution.
3. Eligible counterparties: an investment firm; a credit institution; an insurance company; a collective investment scheme authorised under the UCITS directive or its management company; a pension fund or its management company; another regulated financial institution; a national government; a central bank; a supranational organisation.[21]

The important thing to keep in mind is that professional clients and eligible counterparties have the right to opt-out of CASS protection, whereas retail clients must always be provided with CASS protection.[22]

---

[21] CASS 1.2.8

[22] CASS 7.10.12

## Title transfer collateral arrangements

A Title Transfer Collateral Arrangement is an agreement under which collateral is provided by one party (the Collateral Provider) to the other (the Collateral Receiver) on a title transfer basis.
This means that the Collateral Receiver receives full title (e.g. legal ownership) to that collateral from the Collateral Provider. [23]

Some firms receive and post cash as collateral on behalf of the clients they manage. Asset managers for example, have long given prime brokers custody of their funds' cash, as well as securities, with full rights allowing the prime broker to do as it wants with the cash, on the understanding that the prime brokers will provide attractive terms.

If a client posts collateral by title transfer – which they do, in securities lending, repo and swap transactions – the cash belongs wholly to the prime broker.

Title transfer is only available to professional clients or eligible counterparties. Retail clients cannot use title transfer. [24]

Under the client money rules, the prime broker needs to secure written consent from its clients, the fund, to confirm that the client understands the nature of the transaction and the risks it represents. [25]

*[handwritten: prime broker → help hedge-funds handle large investment transfers]*

---

[23] CASS 7.11.1
[24] CASS 7.11.1
[25] CASS 7.11.3

## Rehypothecation

Rehypothecation is also known as repledging or reuse. It is the practice of a firm that has received collateral 'reusing' that collateral with a third party. This is essentially the firm reusing the collateral for its own purposes. The benefit to the client that originally provided the collateral is usually lower costs.

The collapses of both Lehman Brothers and MF Global highlighted the need for of strong records and controls when rehypothecating assets. Rehypothecation of client assets is only permitted when a 'right to use' clause is in place or the client has transferred full legal ownership.

## Right to Use' clauses

A firm has the right to rehypothecate collateral if the right of use has been agreed with client.

When rehypothecating collateral under the right to use clause, the firm is still under obligation to replace the original collateral with an equivalent financial instrument when the original collateral that the client provided is no longer required to meet the client's obligations.

For retail clients, the firm should ensure:

1. The client is notified that full ownership of the money has been transferred to the firm and, as such, the client no longer has a proprietary claim over this money and the firm can deal with it on its own right
2. The transfer is for the purposes of securing or covering the client's obligations

SECTION 2: CASS REQUIREMENTS AND BEST PRACTICE

**3.** An equivalent transfer is made back to the client if the provision of collateral by the client is no longer necessary

**4.** There is a reasonable link between the timing and the amount of the collateral transfer and the obligation that the client owes, or is likely to owe, to the firm.[26]

## Bare security interests

If a client places collateral with a firm that has no right to use clause or full title transfer, then the firm is not permitted to reuse the assets.[27] This is known as a bare security interest. The client would remain the legal owner of the asset until a liability crystallises.

---

**26** CASS 7.2.7 &
**27** CASS 3.1.3

# SECTION 3:
# KEY PILLARS OF CASS REGULATIONS

## SECTION 3: KEY PILLARS OF CASS REGULATIONS

There are four key pillars of CASS regulation:

**(1)**
**Identification**

**(2)**
**Segregation**

**(3)**
**Reconciliation**

**(4)**
**Record-keeping**

# CHAPTER 3.1: IDENTIFICATION

The key pillar of identification is being able to separate client money and assets from the firm's own assets. In practical terms this means being aware of all scenarios in which client money and assets can occur within the firm's business model and ensuring that the client money or assets is captured and separated.

**Discharge of fiduciary duty**

Money ceases to be client money when:

- The firm pays money into a bank account in the name of the client, if the clients have instructed or consented to the payment
- Client money is paid to a third party when the firm is obliged to do so under an applicable law (e.g. to HMRC)
- Client money is transferred under the 'transfer of business' rules, by operation of a transfer clause in client agreements
- Where client money is paid to charity under the unclaimed client money/de minimis rules.[1]

---

[1] CASS 7.11.34

SECTION 3: KEY PILLARS OF CASS REGULATIONS

## CHAPTER 3.2: SEGREGATION

The key pillar of segregation is ensuring that client money is adequately segregated when it arises.

### Approach to segregation

There are two approaches to segregation.

Under the normal approach, firms receiving any client money must segregate it promptly into client money bank accounts.

The alternative approach allows firms not to segregate client money on receipt (i.e., not receive it into a client bank account, and to have until the end of the next business day to decide whether or they need to segregate it or pay it out).[2]

### The normal approach to segregation – immediate segregation

The normal approach to segregation requires firms to receive client money directly into a client bank account (unless the firms are using the alternative approach to client money segregation)[3], meaning that these firms should not first receive any client money into the firm's own accounts.

This does not stop firms from making payments from their own accounts into their client bank accounts when, for example, such sums are due and payable by the firm to the client. [4]

---

2 CASS 7.13.5
3 CASS 7.13.6
4 CASS 7.13.39

A firm should promptly, and in any event no later than one business day after the money becomes due and payable, either pay the money to the client or segregate that money in a client bank account.[5]

Unless the firm uses the alternative approach, all client money must be received directly into a client bank account and may not be received via the firm's own accounts. [6]

Firms should ensure that clients and any third parties make transfers of any money which will be client money, directly into the firm's client bank accounts.

Firms must establish procedures whereby client monies received into firm accounts are returned, with a request for payment to the appropriate client bank account.
This may involve the communication of amended settlement instructions.

Firms may continue to make payments from their own accounts to client bank accounts in respect of any sum which is due and payable to the client from the firm. [7]

The client money rules do not prevent a firm from receiving money from clients via a payment service provider. However, if a firm uses or is considering using a payment service provider, it should consider how this will impact on all its obligations under the client money rules.

For example, a firm may wish to make use of the prudent segregation rules to mitigate the risk of using one client's money for another client's trades.

---

[5] CASS 7.13.31

[6] CASS 7.13.6

[7] CASS 7.13.39

## Immediate segregation – members of recognised central counterparties (CCPs)

Firms must use 'reasonable endeavours' to ensure that their arrangements with Central Counterparties (CCPs) enable them to make and receive payments relating to the firm's business into and out of the firm's bank accounts, and those relating to client payments into or out of client bank accounts.[8]

If this segregation cannot be achieved, 'mixed' amounts must be paid into or out of the firm's bank accounts. This is to minimise the risk of client money being used to cover margin calls on proprietary accounts at the CCP.[9]

The client money element of a mixed payment received into the house account must be paid into a client bank account promptly and in any event by the close of business of the next business day following receipt.[10]

Firms will be required to maintain a prudent segregation of client money (mandatory prudent segregation amount' (MPSA) in their client bank accounts. This is to address the risk that on any given day insufficient client money is held in client bank accounts as a result of the client money element of the mixed payment being received into, and held for a period in, the firm account.[11]

Firms are required to review the MPSA amount that they hold at least quarterly. They have a period of 10 business days

---

[8] CASS 7.13.71

[9] CASS 7.13.72

[10] CASS 7.13.72

[11] CASS 7.13.73

to carry out each review and to complete any adjustments to the MPSA in the client bank account.[12]

## The alternative approach to segregation

The alternative approach to segregation allows firms to not segregate client money on receipt.[13]

Prior to adopting the alternative approach to client money segregation, firms are required to:

- Establish and document the reasons for using the alternative approach, on a per-business line basis, prior to first adopting the alternative approach for a particular business line[14]
- Notify the FCA three months in advance of its intention to adopt the alternative approach[15]
- Obtain a report from an independent auditor in respect of the firm's proposed use of the alternative approach.[16]

A firm is required to review at least annually its reasons for continuing to operate the alternative approach for each business line.[17]

## Alternative approach – auditor assurances

Prior to adopting the alternative approach to client money segregation, a firm must obtain a report from an independent

---

[12] CASS 7.13.73
[13] CASS 7.13.54
[14] CASS 7.13.55
[15] CASS 7.13.57
[16] CASS 7.13.58
[17] CASS 7.13.59

auditor in respect of the firm's proposed use of the alternative approach.

The auditor must opine on two matters:

1. Whether the firm's systems and controls are adequately designed to enable the firm to use the alternative approach effectively for each business line.
2. Whether the firm's proposed method of calculating and maintaining the 'mandatory prudent segregation amount' is adequately designed to enable the firm to comply with the rules relating to the cash buffer. [18]

## Alternative approach - Mandatory Prudent Segregation Amount

Firms operating the alternative approach will be required to calculate and maintain a prudent segregation of client money (mandatory prudent segregation amount' (MPSA) in their client bank accounts.

This is to address the risk that on any given day insufficient client money is held in client bank accounts as a result of the client money element of the mixed payment being received into, and held for a period in, the firm account. [19]
When calculating the MPSA a firm must take into account:

- The client money requirement
- The daily adjustment payments that the firm makes into, or removes from, its client bank account
- The amount of money received by the firm in its own

---

[18] CASS 7.13.58

[19] CASS 7.13.65

bank account which it did not initially identify as part of its client money requirement, but which subsequently, and during that prior period, became part of its client money requirement
- The impact of any particular events
- The seasonal nature of a business line or any other aspect of a business line on the client money requirement, the daily adjustment payments that the firm makes into its client bank account and the unidentified credits over the forthcoming three months.

Firms are required to use the previous three months' trading records to calculate the MPSA and they must review the MPSA amount at least quarterly.[20]

Firms are also required to create and maintain an 'alternative approach record'. This records the dates on which the firm determines each MPSA amount, the dates and amounts of payments into and withdrawals from client bank accounts to adjust the MPSA and the fact that the payment or withdrawal was made in accordance with the MPSA rules.[21]

## Alternative approach – intra-day adjustments

Firms using the alternative approach are permitted to adjust the balance of client money they hold in client bank accounts before they complete a client money reconciliation.

During the course of carrying out an internal client money reconciliation (on T0), the rules permit a firm to increase the balance held in its client bank accounts if (and only if) the firm reasonably expects the client money requirement for

---

[20] CASS 7.13.65
[21] CASS 7.13.67

the previous business day (T-1) will increase above the client money resource currently (at T0) held in the client bank accounts.

The firm may only form such expectations on the basis of the internal client money reconciliation calculation that it is in the process of carrying out (relating to T-1).

Similarly, if on the basis of the internal client money reconciliation calculation that the firm is in the process of carrying out on T0 (relating to T-1), the firm reasonably expects the client money requirement for the previous business day (T-1) to decrease below the client money resource currently (at T0) held in the client bank accounts, the firm may make intra-day transfers out of the client bank accounts.

However, in doing so, the firm must act prudently and manage the risk of not having segregated sufficient client money resources that reflect its actual client money requirement.

If a firm chooses to make intra-day transfers under this rule, the transfers must be linked to the internal client money reconciliation calculation that it is in the process of carrying out. [22]

### Acknowledgement letters

Before a firm holds client money it is required to send and receive back a signed acknowledgement letter[23] that states:

- The bank or any other counterparty that the client money is held with do not have any recourse or right against that client money.

---

[22] CASS 7.13.63
[23] CASS 7.18.2

- The title of the account contains the word 'client' and is different to the title of any other account containing money that belongs to the firm.[24]

For client money acknowledgement letters, there is a standard wording that the firm must follow.[25]

For central counterparties this process is a one-way notification. The protections which would otherwise be safeguarded through a two-way acknowledgment letter process are achieved directly through the requirements placed on CCPs under EMIR, although enhanced by the provision of a one-way notification.[26]

## Acknowledgement letter requirements

Acknowledgement letters must be drafted on the letterhead of the firm.

Client money firms must periodically, and on at least an annual basis, review their acknowledgement letters and promptly arrange for a replacement acknowledgement letter whenever they become aware of an inaccuracy, or if an account is transferred to a new entity (for instance if there is a merger or sale of the business).

Client money firms must also use reasonable endeavours to ensure that any individual that has countersigned an acknowledgment letter was authorised to do so (i.e. obtain from their counterparties a list of their authorised signatories).

---

[24] CASS 7.18.1
[25] CASS 7.18.6
[26] CASS 7.18.4

Acknowledgement letters must be kept for a minimum of five years after closure of the accounts to which they relate.[27]

## Acknowledgement letters - Authorised Central Counterparties (CCP)

A specific acknowledgement template gives the CCP the option of countersigning and returning the acknowledgement letter, however this is not a requirement.

A firm can use a client transaction account with a CCP at any time after providing the CCP with the relevant acknowledgment letter, whether or not the CCP has countersigned and returned the letter to the firm.

Although the CCP does not have to acknowledge receipt of the letter, firms must ensure that these letters continue to be issued when required, in order to maintain compliance.[28]

Firms are also required to ensure they have an acknowledgment letter in place to cover any client money placed into an overnight money market deposit *before* that deposit is made.[29]

A firm may complete and execute an acknowledgment letter with a bank before it places client money into overnight money market deposits by setting out in the body of the letter:

- The title and other account information for the client bank account from which the deposits will be placed

---

[27] CASS 7 Annex 2 Client bank account acknowledgment letter template
[28] CASS 7.18.4
[29] CASS 7.13.15

- How the firm will notify the bank that the money market deposit being placed with it consists of client money (eg by inclusion of the words 'client money deposit' in its instructions to the bank). [30]

## Custody asset registration

Firm's must generally register custody assets in the name of the client or a nominee which is controlled by the firm or the firm's group.

Firms are generally prohibited from registering their own assets in the same name as the safe custody assets they hold for clients. It is permitted in two specific situations:

1. Where doing so arises incidentally to the investment business the firm carries on for the account of a client or to other steps taken by the firm to comply with the custody rules
2. Where doing so arises only as a result of the law or market practice of a jurisdiction outside of the UK. [31]

Correct registration reduces the risk of custody assets being misappropriated, or client's rights in those assets being lost or diminished.

## Custodian agreement

Before a firm holds custody assets, it is required to send and receive back a signed custodian agreement. This agreement must state that the binding terms of the arrangement between the firm and the relevant third party will be in force

---

**30** CASS 7.13.16

**31** CASS 6.2.3

# SECTION 3: KEY PILLARS OF CASS REGULATIONS

for the duration for that arrangement. It should also clearly set out the custody service(s) that third party is contracted to provide. [32]

A 'lien' is the right given over assets to repay debts. A firm should generally ensure that any agreement with a third party does not include a lien unless it is a requirement of the jurisdiction in which the asset is held, or is confined to charges arising from custody services specifically related to safe custody assets in the account.

## Client money held by third parties

If a third party holds money for a client of the firm (rather than a client of the third party), that money remains client money of the firm and the firm should include the amount in its internal client money reconciliations.

When undertaking an internal client money reconciliation, firms are required to include sums of client money that they allow another person to hold in a client transaction account.[33]

## Client money relating to custody assets held by custodians

Firms that hold custody assets and deposit these with third parties must recognise any money derived from these assets as client money (where appropriate).[34] The money should therefore be held in a client bank account in the name of the firm. This could be at the custodian itself if the custodian is a bank.

As an alternative, the firm and the third party can establish a contractual agreement to cover the holding of client money

---

[32] CASS 6.3.4A

[33] CASS 7.16.27

[34] CASS 7.14.5

by the third party in a client transaction account, showing that it is holding the money on behalf of the firm's clients.[35]

If the firm uses the banking exemption, they must have systems and controls in place to ensure that they recognise this money as being held under the banking exemption, or if held by a third party, as client money.

## Allocation of client money

Firms are required to allocate client money receipts to an individual client promptly, and within ten business days of receipt.

They must record this client money as 'unallocated client money' while working to allocate the payment.[36]

Where a firm is unable to identify whether money it receives is client money or its own money, it must treat this as 'unidentified client money' while taking all necessary steps to determine its status.

Firms should segregate the amount reasonably believed to represent client money as client money, while working to allocate the unidentified payment.[37]

If firms cannot identify whether money received is client money or the firms' money, they should consider whether it should be returned to the payer.

Firms need to document the circumstances under which unidentified money is returned to the sender.[38]

---

**35** CASS 7.14.6

**36** CASS 7.13.36

**37** CASS 7.13.37

**38** CASS 7.13.38

SECTION 3: KEY PILLARS OF CASS REGULATIONS

## Unclaimed custody assets and client money

If firms have client assets and money that have not been claimed by clients, and they wish to offload this money and assets, they are required to take reasonable steps to trace the clients.

After determining, as far as reasonably possible, the current contact details for a client, a firms is expected to attempt to communicate with that client three times before disposing of the client's unclaimed monies or assets.
This procedure is not be available for an unclaimed custody asset until after at least 12 years and for unclaimed client money until after at least six years. [39]

If the clients cannot be traced, firms are permitted to pay away these monies and assets to charity. Firms are not obliged, however, to pay away any unclaimed client money balances and can choose to maintain them indefinitely.

For unclaimed client assets that are paid away to charity, firms are required to unconditionally undertake to make good any valid claim.[40] Firms that do decide to pay away unclaimed client money should consider whether to insure against future valid claims being made against their own funds.

For de-minimis amounts of up to £25 for retail clients and £100 for professional clients, an abbreviated procedure can be followed. Here, the balance may be paid away 28 days after the firm has attempted to contact the client at least once, using the most up-to-date contact details.[41]

---

**39** CASS 7.11.50 & CASS 6.2.10
**40** CASS 7.11.54 & CASS 6.2.14
**41** CASS 7.11.57

Firms should have procedures and policies in place for paying away unclaimed client money to ensure that these are consistent with the rules.

## Unclaimed custody assets

Firms may either pay unclaimed custody assets to charity or liquidate those assets and pay the proceeds to charity.

This procedure is not available for an unclaimed custody asset until at least 12 years since the firm last received instructions concerning any custody assets from or on behalf of the client.[42]

Firms are required to follow 'reasonable steps' to trace the client concerned and to return the safe custody asset. They should determine, as far as reasonably possible, the current contact details for a client and attempt to communicate with that client three times before disposing of the client's assets.[43]

Firms should follow the same 'reasonable steps' set out previously in respect of unclaimed client money balances. However, they should not wait until the end of this 12-year period to ensure they are holding up-to-date contact details for their clients.

Firms must also ensure that paying away custody assets in this way would be consistent with the arrangements under which it holds such assets and is permitted by law.

Firms should review and amend their procedures and policies for paying away unclaimed custody assets to ensure that these are consistent with the new rules.

---

[42] CASS 6.2.10
[43] CASS 6.2.10

SECTION 3: KEY PILLARS OF CASS REGULATIONS

## Unclaimed client money

Firms may pay unclaimed client money to charity or liquidate those assets and pay the proceeds to charity. This procedure is not available for unclaimed client money until at least six years since the firm last received instructions concerning any client money from or on behalf of the client. [44]

Firms are required to follow 'reasonable steps' to trace the client concerned and to return the balance. They should determine, as far as reasonably possible, the current contact details for a client and attempt to communicate with that client three times before disposing of the client's assets. [45]

Firms should follow the same 'reasonable steps' set out previously in respect of unclaimed client money balances. However, they should not wait until the end of this six-year period to ensure they are holding up-to-date contact details for their clients.

Firms must also ensure that paying away client money in this way would be consistent with the arrangements under which it holds such assets and is permitted by law.

Firms should review and amend their procedures and policies for paying away unclaimed client money to ensure that these are consistent with the new rules.

## Unclaimed custody assets and client money

Any costs the firm incurs must be paid out of the firm's own funds. This includes any costs the firm incurs in:

---

[44] CASS 7.11.50
[45] CASS 6.2.10

- Tracing a client
- Liquidating unclaimed assets
- Arranging transfer of unclaimed balances, liquidation proceeds or unclaimed assets to clients
- Obtaining insurance to cover any claims arising from the actions the firm may undertake under these rules. This approach is consistent with the responsibilities firms generally have to their clients as a consequence of holding their monies and assets, including, where appropriate, those firms' duties as trustee. [46]

## Unclaimed client money – de minimis threshold

There is a de minimis threshold for unclaimed client money of up to £25 for retail clients and £100 for other clients.[47]

## Unbreakable term deposits

Under CASS 7, the maximum period that cash can be held in an unbreakable term deposit is 95 days. This is in order to ensure that in the event of an insolvency, money can be returned as quickly as possible. [48]

## Interest

A firm must pay a retail client any interest earned on client money held for that client, unless it has otherwise notified them in writing.[49]

---

[46] CASS 7.11.58 & CASS 6.2.16
[47] CASS 7.11.57
[48] CASS 7.13.13
[49] CASS 7.11.32

The firm may, under the terms of its agreement with the client, pay some, none, or all interest earned to the relevant client.[50]

So in summary, as long as a firm discloses to the client how it will treat interest received on the client money, it is possible to:

- Keep it all as a margin
- Pay it all to the clients; or
- Retain a proportion of the interest and pay the remainder to the clients.

Client agreements need to be specific about payment dates and rates.

## Commission rebate

If a firm has agreed to rebate commissions to specific clients, those rebates are required to be treated as client money when they become due and payable to the client, as stated in the client agreement.

## Physical receipts

Firms that receive client money in the form of cash, cheque, or other physical means must bank it into a client money bank account promptly, and no later than one business day after receipt.

If a firm is unable to pay physical client money received into a client bank account within one business day after receipt because of regulatory or other restrictions, it must record the receipt in its books, hold it in a secure location and deposit it as soon as possible.[51]

---

**50** CASS 7.11.33
**51** CASS 7.13.32

If a firm receives a post-dated cheque, it must keep it in a secure location, record its receipt in its books and records, and the cheque must be deposited in a client bank account by no later than the date on the cheque (if that is a business day or, if not, the next business day after the date on the cheque).[52]

Firms should ensure that they have a secure location, such as a safe, for holding client money awaiting banking. Firms should have a documented reconciliation procedure in respect of receipts held prior to banking.

## Cheques

Current-dated cheques that cannot be banked on the day of receipt must be recorded and held securely until the following working day, when they must be banked or returned.[53]

The FCA considers cheques to be paid in 'on acceptance' at the bank.[54]

Firms should carefully consider their processes, including their contractual arrangements with clients. Prudent segregation may also be required to fund cheques that are not banked in a prompt manner.

The industry standards for sterling cheque clearances are as follows:

- Deposit Day + 2 working days – cheque is cleared for interest.
- Deposit Day + 4 working days – cheque is cleared for withdrawal.

---

[52] CASS 7.13.33
[53] CASS 7.13.32
[54] CASS 7.11.40

- Deposit Day + 6 working days – cheque is cleared for fate and cannot bounce.
- Some banks will offer commercial propositions to enable their clients to withdraw funds prior to Deposit Day + 4. Firms may wish to check the commercial arrangements they have with their bank.

## Cleared funds

Firms should ensure that their systems and procedures ensure that:

- Client money received from a client has cleared, before trades are carried out in respect of the sums received.
- Client money received from a sale has cleared before any payment is made to the client.[55]

In scenarios where this is not possible, an intra-day risk is created.

## Settlement

When a transaction is undertaken for an asset, there is always an agreed settlement date (also known as the contractual settlement date) when the money and/or assets are due to be exchanged.

However, the agreed settlement date may differ from the actual settlement date when the exchange of money and/or assets actually takes place. The difference between the agreed settlement date and the actual settlement date can be different due to various reasons, for example the seller

---

[55] CASS 7.12.3

may not have the asset on the agreed settlement date.

When considering settlement, practitioners should be aware of the two different types of settlement and their implications on CASS.

The client agreement should state when the assets and cash will be added or removed from the client's account.

Contractual settlement refers to an agreement stating that the assets and cash will be added or removed from the client's account on the agreed settlement date. This is the standard arrangement. It means that the firm is required to segregate equivalent client assets from the agreed settlement date, regardless of whether actual settlement has occurred.

## Intra-day risk

A key principle of CASS is that client money is held according to statutory trust requirements. A firm is not permitted, in its capacity as trustee, to allow one client's money to fund another client's transactions.

The FCA has said that *"Peter's money should not be used to fund Paul's transactions"*[56].

The risk that one client's money is used to fund another client's transactions is generally referred to as a CASS 'intra-day risk'.

A risk of shortfall can arise through many different scenarios, for example:

- Internal systems failures

---

[56] PS 14/9 paragraph 7.133

SECTION 3: KEY PILLARS OF CASS REGULATIONS

- Banking systems failures
- Transaction settlement fails
- Intra-day exposure between the receipt and payment of client money
- Bounced cheques
- Rejected direct debits
- BACS payments which leave the account before expected receipts arrive.

The most popular methods to minimise intraday risk are pre-funding and prudent segregation.

### Intra-day shortfall example

An example of intra-day shortfall is when a firm is required to make payments to clients from its client money bank account once trades for those clients settle into that account:

- Trades may settle throughout the day, however payments to clients are all released by BACS in the morning.
- As the firm in this example operates a pooled account, BACS payments are released prior to the trade settlements reaching the pooled account.
- Hence the BACS payments have been made with money that was already in the pooled account, i.e. other client's money.

In this example it may be possible to prefund the settlement value prior to the BACS payments, as the exact amount is known. If there is sufficient time the pre-funding can be placed prior to the BACS payments.

Alternatively, a calculated prudent segregation amount

could be retained in the client bank account to cover these shortfalls.

## Pre-funding

There is no definition of pre-funding within the rules, but the mere fact that a payment has been made from a firm's own funds to the client money account does not necessarily make the payment a prudent segregation.

Pre-funding generally takes place when a specific event has been identified that will cause a quantifiable shortfall, in which it is possible to identify which clients' business will lead to the shortfall.

There are benefits to pre-funding.

It is flexible, as it can be used to respond to specific events rather than a more formal prudent segregation process. It is less costly, as it only ties up money for a short period of time rather than indefinitely. It can also be used just for specific amounts – when there is a quantifiable shortfall, the full amount of risk can be covered rather than an amount that covers the average risk.

## Is Pre-funding permitted?

CASS 7.13.47G states: *"examples of the types of risks that a firm may wish to provide protection for under CASS 7.13.41 R [prudent segregation] include systems failures and business that is conducted on non-business days* **where the firm would be unable to pay any anticipated shortfall into its client bank accounts**".

It would therefore appear that the FCA contemplates situations where a firm makes payments into the client money bank account to cover anticipated shortfalls, but the payments do not fall under prudent segregation.

The FCA appear to suggest that payments into the client money bank account to cover anticipated shortfalls, are just one measure that could be taken to address intra-day risk, with prudent segregation being another option.

However, Paragraph 7.137 of PS14/9 is where the confusion lies. It states: *"As set out in the CP, the rules do not prohibit firms using their own money to fund clients' trades (for example, before receiving funds from clients). If the firm wishes to do this through the client account, it may be able to make use of the prudent segregation rules to mitigate the risk of using one client's money for another client's trades. It may instead wish to do so directly from its own bank accounts."*

This implies that funding clients' trades through the client money bank account (before receiving those funds from clients) must be done via prudent segregation or from the firm's house accounts. However this is not a rule nor official guidance and does not explicitly prevent pre-funding.

At numerous industry events the FCA has unofficially stated disapproval for pre-funding but has thus far stopped short of making the disapproval official with guidance or rules.

Due to the lack of rules preventing pre-funding, some firms have implemented pre-funding without punishment. It is therefore advisable to tread carefully if using pre-funding and where possible it is preferable to fund trades using the firm's house account.

I have described some best practice in terms of documentation further below if a firm does indeed choose to use pre-funding as its preferred method of mitigating intra-day risk.

## Prudent segregation

CASS 7.13.41 states that: *"If it is prudent to do so to prevent a shortfall in client money on the occurrence of a primary pooling event, a firm may pay money of its own into a client bank account and subsequently retain that money in the client bank account (prudent segregation). Money that the firm retains in a client bank account under this rule is client money for the purposes of the client money rules and the client money distribution rules".*

Prudent segregation does not require the shortfall to be a likely outcome, nor does it require any certainty as to the amount and timing of such a shortfall, or which specific clients' business will lead to the shortfall.

Prudent segregation should not be used as a solution for poor systems or controls, or bad recordkeeping.

## Prudent segregation and pre-funding documentation

A prudent segregation policy must be supported by a prudent segregation record.
The policy must be approved by the firm's governing body and retained for at least five years after the date it ceases to retain such money as a prudent segregation amount.[57]

A prudent segregation record must be up-to-date and must include specific details on the amount of prudent segregation calculated and the changes to that amount.[58]

The policy should document:

---

[57] CASS 7.13.43
[58] CASS 7.13.50 & CASS 7.13.51

SECTION 3: KEY PILLARS OF CASS REGULATIONS

- The specific anticipated risks that would be prudent for the firm to protect.
- Why the firm considers the use of such a payment to be reasonable for the firm.
- The method the firm will use to calculate the amount of money required.[59]

In respect of pre-funding, a firm must have a clear policy document in place. It should document:

- A best practice approach.
- The same components captured in a prudent segregation policy.
- The reasons a firm has used pre-funding ,rather than funding trades from the house account.
- Approval from firm's governing body.

**Funding trades via a firm's house account**

As discussed above, it is the FCA's preference that funding clients' trades through the client money bank account before receiving those funds from clients is done directly via the firm's house accounts.

It is best practice to document this in an intra-day risk policy that sets out:

- The specific anticipated risks and trades that would be prudent for the firm to fund directly from its house accounts.
- Why the firm considers the use of such funding reasonable for the firm.

---

[59] CASS 7.13.43

- How and when client money related to those anticipated risks and trades will be transferred back to the house accounts when received from the clients.

## Intra-day risk: best practice

With regards to best practice I have set out a range of options that can mitigate intra-day risk, coupled with indications of when it is appropriate to use them:

### Change the processes in place

Changing T&Cs and/or processes to avoid the risk of a shortfall arising. This is best used as a long-term solution when it is financially realistic and the root cause of the issue is the firm's own system and controls.

### Prudent segregation

For exposures when the amounts and/or the timing of the exposures cannot be calculated precisely.

### Pre-funding or funding via house accounts

For exposures where an event has been identified that will cause a quantifiable shortfall.

### Not funding

Establish why a shortfall will *not* arise and justify the rationale for not funding risks. Choosing not to fund and therefore leaving a known risk should only be used if the risk is not significant and the decision has been agreed by a firm's governing body.

## Removing funding

If a firm supplies funding directly from its own bank accounts, for example by paying for transactions from a corporate account, the firm can be repaid from the client's money as and when it becomes available.

The removal of prudent segregation must follow quite specific rules under CASS 7.13.49, which suggest it may only be repayable to the firm at the point of the next reconciliation. It is best practice that money deposited into the client account as pre-funding is also removed at the point of the next reconciliation.

**Intra-day risk records**

All pre-funding, as well as trades via the house account and prudent segregation activity, should be documented and a record should be maintained. When a risk is not funded, the risk should then be tracked and monitored, and this MI should be reviewed by the firm's CASS committee.

## CHAPTER 3.3: RECONCILIATION

The key pillar of reconciliation is regularly ensuring that the client money and custody assets that a firm holds is the amount that should be held.

### Client money reconciliations

Client money firms are required to undertake each of the following reconciliations, where relevant:

1. Internal client money reconciliations:

   a. (When using the normal approach to client money segregation) to check on a daily basis whether its client money resource, as at the close of business the previous business day, was equal to its client money requirement at the close of business on that previous day.[60]

   b. (When using the alternative approach to client money segregation) to ensure on a daily basis that its client money resource, as at the close of business on any day it carries out an internal client money reconciliation, is equal to its client money reconciliation at the close of business on the previous day. [61]

2. External client money reconciliations:

   a. This is a comparison of the balance, currency by currency, on each client bank account and client transaction account as recorded by the firm, with the

---

[60] CASS 7.15.15
[61] CASS 7.15.16

SECTION 3: KEY PILLARS OF CASS REGULATIONS

> balance on that account as set out in the most recent statement or other form of confirmation issued by the bank or person with whom the account is held.[62]

Firms are required to undertake internal client money reconciliations on a daily basis, and external client money reconciliations whenever necessary but on at least a monthly basis.[63]

## Client money reconciliation frequencies

Most firms will be required to undertake a review of the frequency at which they undertake external reconciliations on at least an annual basis. However, firms that already undertake an external client money reconciliation on a daily basis will not be required to separately review this decision unless they choose to change this frequency. [64]

## Internal client money reconciliation

The internal client money reconciliation may be performed by one of the standard methods or a non-standard method[65]:

In the standard method, a firm must calculate its client money requirement by one of two possible methods:

1. Individual client balance, which is available to all firms. This requires a firm to calculate its client money requirement by reference to how much the firm should be holding in total for each of its individual clients, with a

---

[62] CASS 7.15.20
[63] CASS 7.15.22
[64] CASS 7.15.26
[65] CASS 7.15.15

positive balance in respect of non-margined transactions, margined transactions and certain other matters.[66]

2. Net negative add-back, which is only available to CASS 7 asset management firms and CASS loan-based crowdfunding firms, and only when the firm does not engage in any margined transactions for clients. This requires a firm to calculate its client money requirement by reference to the balances in each client bank account, adding back any individual client's net position in a specific client bank account that is negative.[67]

The non-standard method does not meet the requirements placed on firms undertaking one of the standard methods of internal client money reconciliation.[68]

## Non-standard method of internal client money reconciliation

If a firm uses a non-standard method of reconciliation, the firm should consider whether the method achieves the same specified outcome as if the firm had used one of the standard methods.

This includes considering whether the method will:

- Check whether the amount of client money recorded in the firm's records as being segregated in client bank accounts meets the firm's obligation to its clients under the client money rules on a daily basis (when using the normal approach to client money segregation).

---

[66] CASS 7.16.16

[67] CASS 7.16.17

[68] CASS 7.15.17

SECTION 3: KEY PILLARS OF CASS REGULATIONS

- Calculate, on a daily basis, the amount of client money to be segregated in a client bank account which meets a firm's obligations to its clients under the client money rules (when using the alternative approach to client money segregation).[69]

Before a firm uses a non-standard method of reconciliation the firm must obtain a report from its auditor stating whether:

- The firm's proposals for a non-standard method of internal client money reconciliation is adequately designed to provide an equivalent degree of protection to one of the standard methods of internal client money reconciliation; and
- The firm's systems and controls are adequately designed to enable it to operate effectively the non-standard method the firm proposes to use. [70]

---

**69** CASS 7.15.18
**70** CASS 7.15.18

# Internal reconciliation net negative method example

CASS 7 Net Negative

| Resource | |
|---|---|
| **(1) Bank balances** | |
| Client Bank Account 1 | £37,503.85 |
| Client Bank Account 2 | £27,000.00 |
| **Aggregate bank balances** | **£64,503.85** |
| **Resource available** | **£64,503.85** |
| Requirement | |
| **(2) Bank balances** | |
| Client Bank Account 1 | £37,503.85 |
| Client Bank Account 2 | £27,000.00 |
| **Aggregate bank balances** | **£64,503.85** |
| **(3) Adjustment for Negative Balances** | **£0.00** |
| **(4) Adjustment for Prudent Segregation** | **£0.00** |
| **Requirement to cover** | **£64,503.85** |
| **Resource** | **£64,503.85** |
| **Surplus/deficit** | **£0.00** |
| **Internal Control Check** | |
| Amount related to individual client balances | £44,503.85 |
| Prudent Segregation | £5,400.00 |
| Unallocated client Money Where Not Already Included | £4,600.00 |
| Unidentified client Money Where Not Already Included | £4,400.00 |
| Money at third Parties, where applicable | £3,300.00 |
| Negative Client Balances | £2,300.00 |
| Cheques Received Not Yet Banked, Where Already Posted | £0.00 |
| Total | £64,503.85 (reconciles with requirement) |

# Internal reconciliation individual client balance method example

CASS 7 Client Balance

| Resource | |
|---|---|
| (1) Bank balances | |
| Client Bank Account 1 | £377,503.85 |
| Client Bank Account 2 | £27,000.00 |
| Aggregate bank balances | £64,503.85 |
| Resource available | £64.503.85 |
| Requirement | |
| (2) Client Free Money | £44,102.85 |
| (3) Sales delivered by client unpaid to client | £0.00 |
| (4) Purchases paid by client undelivered to client | £0.00 |
| (5) Less Purchases delivered to client unpaid by client | £0.00 |
| (6) Unpaid fees | £0.00 |
| (7) Negative Client Balances | £5,401.00 |
| (8) Unallocated Client Money | £2,478.00 |
| (9) Unidentified Client Money | £2,522.00 |
| (10) Prudent Segregation Amount | £9,457.06 |
| (11) Asset Shortfall Funding Adjustment | £0.00 |
| (12 Cheques issued not cashed | £942.96 |
| Requirement to cover | £64,903.87 |
| Resource | £64,503.85 |
| Surplus/deficit | -£400.02 |

# Internal reconciliation individual client balance method example (Margin Transaction Requirement)

CASS 7 Client Balance MTR

| Resource | |
|---|---|
| (1) Bank balances | |
| Client Bank Account 1 | £377,503.85 |
| Client Bank Account 2 | £27,000.00 |
| Aggregate bank balances | £64,503.85 |
| Resource available | £64,503.85 |
| Requirement | |
| (2) Client Free Money | £19,102.85 |
| (3) Positive client's equity balances | £18,209.63 |
| (4) Proportion of individual negative client equity balance secured by client approved collateral | £5,872.8 |
| (5) Firm's net aggregate equity balance on client transaction accounts | £1,372.38 |
| (6) Sales delivered by client unpaid to client | £0.00 |
| (7) Purchases paid by client undelivered to client | £0.00 |
| (8) Less: Purchases delivered to client unpaid by client | £0.00 |
| (9) Unpaid fees | £0.00 |
| (10) Negative Client Balances | £5,401.00 |
| (11) Unallocated Client Money | £2,478.00 |
| (12) Unidentified Client Money | £2,522.00 |
| (13) Prudent Segregation Amount | £9,457.06 |
| (14) Asset Shortfall funding Adjustment | £0.00 |
| (15) Cheques Issued not cashed | £942.96 |
| Requirement to cover | £65,358.68 |
| Resource | £64,503.85 |
| Surplus/deficit | -£854.83 |

## reconciliation discrepancies

[A firm should] determine the reason for any discrepancy between its client money requirement and client money resource, which it identifies as a result of its internal client money reconciliation. It should address any associated shortfall or excess on the same day that it undertakes the internal reconciliation.[71]

The firm should also immediately investigate, and take all reasonable steps to correct, any discrepancy it identifies as a result of its external client money reconciliation (segregating in the interim an amount of client money or approved collateral based on whichever record, or set of records, indicates a greater amount should be held by the firm).[72]

## Custody reconciliations

Firms with safe custody assets are required to undertake each of the following reconciliations:

1. Internal custody record checks (all firms) - Checks as to whether the firm's internal records and accounts of the custody assets held by the firm correspond with the firm's obligations to clients to hold those custody assets. These checks are performed by one of two methods - internal custody reconciliation method or internal system evaluation method.[73]

2. Physical asset reconciliations (all firms that physically hold custody assets) - Comparisons between a firm's internal records and a count of the actual physical safe

---

71 CASS 7.15.29

72 CASS 7.15.31

73 CASS 6.6.11 & CASS 6.6.13

custody assets held by the firm for its clients, performed by one of two methods - total count method or rolling stock method.[74]

3. External custody reconciliations (all firms that either deposit or otherwise register custody assets with a third party) – Reconciliations between a firm's internal accounts and records of custody assets and those of any third parties by whom those custody assets are held or registered.

4. Internal custody record checks, using one of two different methods:

    a. Internal custody reconciliation method - a comparison on a particular date between two separately maintained records:
    
    - A 'client-specific safe custody asset record'
    - An 'aggregate safe custody asset record' – an internal record or account of all the custody assets that the firm holds for clients.[75]

5. Internal system evaluation method - Establishing and running a process to evaluate:

    a. the completeness and accuracy of the firm's internal records and accounts of custody assets held by the firm for clients, in particular whether sufficient information is being completed and accurately recorded by the firm to enable it to identify the custody assets held by the firm for each particular client (i.e. comply with its obligation to maintain a client-specific safe custody asset record), and readily

---

[74] CASS 6.6.22

[75] CASS 6.6.16 & CASS 6.6.17

determine all the custody assets that the firm holds for its clients; and

b. whether the firm's systems and controls correctly identify and resolve all discrepancies in its internal records and accounts of custody assets held by the firm for clients.[76]

## Physical asset reconciliations

There are two different methods for the physical asset reconciliation:

1. 'Total count method' - the count of all physical custody assets held by the firm on a particular date.[77]

2. 'Rolling stock method' - the count of all physical custody assets held by the firm being undertaken in several stages. Each stage refers to a count of a line of stock or group of stock lines (e.g. all the shares with an issuer whose name begins with the letter 'A' or all the stock lines held in connection with a particular business line being counted at the same time).[78]

## Custody reconciliation frequencies

Firms must undertake a physical asset reconciliation as often as necessary, but at least every six months.[79]

Firms are required to undertake internal and external custody reconciliations as regularly as is necessary, but on at least a monthly basis.[80]

---

[76] CASS 6.6.19
[77] CASS 6.6.27
[78] CASS 6.6.29
[79] CASS 6.6.22
[80] CASS 6.6.11 & CASS 6.6.37

Firms are required to review, on at least an annual basis, the frequency at which they undertake reconciliations unless they have already undertake a specific reconciliation daily.[81]

## Handling discrepancies and shortfalls in custody assets

Where a firm identifies a discrepancy between its or any relevant third party's records as a result of custody reconciliations, the firm is required to promptly investigate the reason for discrepancy and resolve that discrepancy without undue delay.[82]

A discrepancy should not be considered to be resolved until the firm is holding the correct amount of custody assets and its records.[83]

Where a discrepancy gives rise to a shortfall in the custody assets the firm should be holding, this will necessitate the firm to make good that shortfall (e.g. by obtaining assets to replace any custody assets which are missing).

If the firm does not immediately make good the shortfall, and it is unable to conclude that another person is responsible for the discrepancy, it is required to cover the shortfall in the interim with either its own assets or an equivalent value of money, until it is able to resolve the underlying discrepancy.[84]

In certain circumstances, firms may also need to consider whether to inform affected clients of the shortfall (for instance

---

[81] CASS 6.6.46
[82] CASS 6.6.49
[83] CASS 6.6.48
[84] CASS 6.6.54

# SECTION 3: KEY PILLARS OF CASS REGULATIONS

if the firm is informed by a third party of the loss of a custody asset).[85]

Where a firm is obliged to cover a shortfall until the discrepancy which gave rise to the shortfall is resolved, and chooses to do this by segregating its own money as client money, the firm will also need to ensure that the relevant clients affected by the shortfall are entitled to protection under the client money rules and that the firm has the relevant permissions to hold client money before it may segregate an amount of its own money as client money.[86]

Firms must ensure that they have systems and controls in place to enable compliance with the client money rules in respect of that money, and to ensure that any client to whom the shortfall is attributable would be entitled to client money protection.

Firms must ensure that their policies and procedures outline how the firm will meet the requirements to make good any shortfalls.

Firms should also check their own client money permissions and ensure that any amounts they transfer for this purpose would only be available for clients' benefit in the event of the firm's failure. These must be clearly recorded.

Firms which normally operate under the 'banking exemption', or that use title transfer collateral arrangements for monies received or held on behalf of clients, will need to ensure that there are appropriate systems and controls in in place to hold client money in compliance with the client money rules.

If a firm in these circumstances wishes to use its own money

---

[85] CASS 6.6.55
[86] CASS 6.6.54

to cover shortfalls in custody assets, then it may need to repaper its agreements or other documentation with the client concerned, to ensure that money may be held for the client's benefit as client money. [87]

Where a firm segregates its own money as client money to cover a custody shortfall, it will need to revisit the valuation each day to ensure it is still segregating the correct amount to cover the shortfall. These assets will then form part of the custody assets included in the firm's next internal custody record check.[88]

## Reconciliations: best practice

The CF10a or senior manager with responsibility for CASS operational oversight should fully understand the process, from delivering files to closing off the reconciliation. Reconciliations should be entity specific.

The basis on which you complete your reconciliations should be recorded, and if the reconciliation is not undertaken daily, the frequency should be reviewed annually.

Archived reconciliations should be retrievable and cover the past five years[89].

Shortfall policy and procedures should be documented.

---

[87] CASS 6.6.54
[88] CASS 6.6.56
[89] CASS 6.6.7 & CASS 7.15.5

# CHAPTER 3.4: RECORD-KEEPING

The key pillar of record-keeping ensures that a firm maintains adequate records to undertake CASS responsibilities.

### Record-keeping – client money

Every firm must maintain its records in a way that allows the firm at any time to promptly determine the total amount of client money it should be holding for each client[90]. 'Promptly' means no later than two business days.[91]

Firms should review their policies and procedures on an ongoing basis, and amend them as required, to ensure that they will comply with any new regulations.

Firms are not required to determine the total amount of client money it holds for each client on an on-going basis, only to ensure that it has the ability to do so within the required timeframe.

### Record-keeping – custody assets

Firms are required to make and retain copies of each custody record check and/or reconciliation the firm undertakes, as well as each review it conducts of these arrangements and its policy and procedures for complying with the FCA's requirements, including those around recordkeeping and reconciliations.

Firms holding custody assets are also required to maintain a client-specific safe custody asset record.

---

**90** CASS 7.15.5

**91** CASS 7.15.6

Firms should review their policies and procedures on an ongoing basis, and amend them as required, to ensure that they will comply with any new regulations.

## Client agreements

Client agreements are a key foundation with regards to CASS compliance. Firms should ensure that:

1. There are clear statements regarding if and when the client's money or assets will or will not have CASS protection in their client agreements.
2. There are clear statements on how interest on client bank accounts will be treated.
3. There are clear statements on how unclaimed custody assets and client money will be treated.
4. They have considered whether the agreements require a clause which allows the firm to transfer the client's money to a third party in the future should the situation arise.
5. Client files and agreements are up-to-date.
6. All client agreements can be located.
7. There is a clear record of how clients are categorised.
8. The firm is able to send ad hoc statements to clients in line with CASS 9.

## Due diligence

The FCA has made it an obligation on firms to undertake appropriate due diligence of third parties that are appointed to hold client money and custody assets.

When a firm makes the selection of third parties that are appointed to hold client money and custody assets they must consider:

- The expertise and market reputation of the third party
- Any legal requirements or market practices related to the holding of client money that could adversely affect clients' rights.[92]

On an ongoing basis the firm should also review:

- The capital of the Capital Requirements Directives (CRD) credit institution Capital Requirements Directives or bank.
- The amount of client money placed, as a proportion of the CRD credit institution or bank's capital and deposits, and, in the case of a qualifying money market fund, compared to any limit the fund may place on the volume of redemptions in any period
- The extent to which client money that the firm deposits or holds with any CRD credit institution or bank incorporated outside the UK would be protected under a deposit protection scheme in the relevant jurisdiction
- The credit-worthiness of the CRD credit institution or bank
- To the extent that the information is available, the level of risk in the investment and loan activities undertaken by the CRD credit institution or bank and affiliated companies.[93]

Additional elements firms should consider in their due diligence are:

---

[92] CASS 6.3.1 & CASS 7.13.10
[93] CASS 6.3.2 & CASS 7.13.11

- Governance and the CF10a role – firms should assess governance the role the CF10a plays at the third party, including committees, project oversight, regulatory change and decision-making. Note – if the third party resides overseas, the CF10a role will not exist.

- Financial stability – when performing an assessment on the financial position of the third party, the firm should focus on the legal entity, however assessing other group members may be useful.

- Operational processes – are there sufficient procedures in place to provide comfort that appropriate controls are in place to safeguard client assets?

- Regulatory – are there sufficient policies and knowledgeable staff in place to meet the existing CASS rule requirements and deal with regulatory changes? Any FCA fines should also be reviewed.

- Contingency – does the third party have a sufficient disaster recovery plan?

- Training – what CASS training is carried out at the third party, who receives it, how frequently is it refreshed and how is this monitored?

## Diversification

To help protect clients against the possible failure of a bank, firms are required to periodically assess whether it is appropriate to diversify (or further diversify) the third parties with which it deposits some or all of the client money that the firm holds.[94]

In carrying out these periodic assessments the firm should consider:

---

[94] CASS 7.13.22

- whether it would be appropriate to deposit client money in client bank accounts opened at a number of third parties
- whether it would be appropriate to limit the amounts of client money it holds with third parties who are in the same group
- whether risks arising from the firm's business models create any need for diversification
- its obligations to arrange adequate protection for client assets
- the outcome of the due diligence it is required to carry out on banks
- the market conditions at the time of the assessment.[95]

Following a periodic assessment, the firm must make any adjustments it concludes are appropriate, either to the third parties it uses and/or to the amounts of client money deposited with each of them.

Firms are also required to record each periodic assessment, including its considerations and conclusions. Firms must keep this record for five years following the conclusion of an assessment.[96]

## Transfer of business

There are two ways in which a firm may transfer client money to a third party in the context of a transfer of business; and in doing so that money will cease to be client money for the

---

[95] CASS 7.13.23
[96] CASS 7.13.25

firm making the transfer:

- It may obtain client consent at the time of the transfer, or include in its client agreement a clause which allows the firm to transfer the client's money to a third party in the future should the situation arise (with notification to the client required).[97]
- If the client holds less than or equal to a de minimis amount of client money per client (£25 for retail clients and £100 for other clients). Consent is not required in this case.[98]

In both cases, the client must be notified within seven days of the transfer taking place[99] and the FCA must be notified seven days before the transfer takes place.[100]

Firms should consider including a transfer clause within their written client agreements. If firms wish to ensure that the option to transfer client money under such a transfer clause is available to them in the future, they can repaper their client agreements with the appropriate wording.

If at the time of transfer a firm does not have such clauses in their client agreements, it is required to obtain the consent of its clients at the time of the transfer and/or apply the 'de minimis' provisions to the extent possible.

In choosing to insert a transfer clause into client agreements, firms are required to commit:

---

[97] CASS 7.11.42
[98] CASS 7.11.44
[99] CASS 7.11.46
[100] CASS 7.11.47

- To transferring the sums to another firm that will hold those sums under the client money rules; or
- To exercising all due skill, care and diligence in assessing whether the person to whom the client money is being transferred will apply adequate measures to protect the sums being transferred.

## Transfer of business – post-transfer notifications

When completing a transfer of business, a firm must ensure that the following notifications are made to clients no later than seven days after the transfer has taken place:

- How the money will be held by the transferee firm.
- The relevant applicable compensation scheme and the option for a client to have transferred sums returned as soon as possible.[101]

Clients may be notified prior to the transfer taking place.

---

101  CASS 7.11.46

# SECTION 4:
# REPORTING REQUIREMENTS

## Annual Notification

Once a year, firms holding client money and/or safe custody assets from investment business are required to determine their CASS classification.

The firm must notify the FCA of its classification within 15 business days of 31 December of the previous calendar year.[1]

Below are the firm classification types[2]:

| CASS firm type | Highest total amount of client money held during the firm's last calendar year or as the case may be that it projects that it will hold during the current calendar year | Highest total value of safe custody assets held by the firm during the firm's last calendar year or as the case may be that it projects that it will hold during the current calendar year |
|---|---|---|
| CASS large firm | More than £1 billion | More than £100 billion |
| CASS medium | An amount equal to or greater than £1 million and less than or equal to £1 billion | An amount equal to or greater than £10 million and less than or equal to £100 billion |
| CASS small firm | Less than £1 million | Less than £10 million |

## Client money and asset return (CMAR)

Client assets sourcebook (CASS) medium and large firms must complete a Client Money and Assets Return (CMAR) each month.[3]

The CMAR gives the FCA an overview of a firm's client money and safe custody assets (client assets) positions and holdings,

---

[1] CASS 1A.2.2
[2] CASS 1A.2.7
[3] CASS 1A.3.1A

as well as a view of the trends in the industry.

This enables the FCA to make regulatory interventions in relation to client assets on a timely, firm-specific or thematic basis.

## CMAR best practice

All CMAR data should be pre-validated, using the same criteria as GABRIEL, the FCA's online system for collecting and storing regulatory data from firms. Validation should ensure consistency between:

- Cash and assets
- One return and the next
- Different systems and suppliers (e.g. what has gone away).

The firm should ensure that all business lines and products are included, and that all figures agree back to totals e.g. client assets/money for the whole business, to ensure completeness.

## CASS resolution pack (CASS RP)

Firms holding client assets from investment business are required to keep certain new and existing documents and records relating to client assets in a CASS Resolution Pack (CASS RP)[4].

The CASS RP ensures documents can be retrieved promptly if the firm fails. It can be held in physical or electronic form.

---

[4] CASS 10.1.1

## SECTION 4: REPORTING REQUIREMENTS

The CASS RP contains documents and records (for example, the latest client money reconciliations and a list of custodians where custody assets are held) that would help an insolvency practitioner (IP) return client assets quickly following an investment firm failure.

The CASS RP should contain, amongst other things:

- A master document with links or information that is sufficient to retrieve all other documents in the CASS RP
- CASS policies and procedures
- A list of institutions holding the relevant client money and custody assets, including contact details
- Written trust acknowledgement letters.
- Written custodian and third-party agreements
- The most recent internal and external reconciliations relating to safe custody assets and client money
- Details of third parties carrying out any outsourced tasks
- Key individuals of the firm involved in CASS processes
- Relevant client agreements.

## CASS RP retrieval timeframes

All documentation forming part the CASS Resolution Pack must be capable of being retrieved within 48 hours of the appointment of an insolvency practitioner or the request of the FCA, irrespective of whether the firm has entered into insolvency[5].

Where documents are held by third parties, the firm must

---

[5] CASS 10.1.7

have adequate arrangements in place to ensure that documents are delivered within the 48-hour timescale.

The FCA notes that the 48-hour period is for retrieval of the relevant documentation and should not be used as a period during which the firm starts to produce the constituent elements of the CASS Resolution Pack[6].

In addition to the 48-hour rule, certain documentation must be able to be retrieved immediately, in order to assist an insolvency practitioner in identifying client assets immediately.[7]

The FCA believes that firms should already have these documents to hand. A full list of the documentation to which the requirement applies is provided below.

| Description | Reference | Retrieval deadline |
|---|---|---|
| Master document containing information sufficient to retrieve each document in the firm's CASS Resolution Pack | CASS 10.2.1R(1) | 48 hours |
| A document identifying institutions appointed by the firm to hold client money or safe custody assets | CASS 10.2.1R(2) | Immediately |
| A document identifying each appointed representative, tied agent, field representative or other agent of the firm that has received client money or safe custody assets in its capacity as the firm's agent | CASS 10.2.1R(3) | 48 hours |

---

**6** CASS 10.1.5

**7** CASS 10.1.9

## SECTION 4: REPORTING REQUIREMENTS

| | | |
|---|---|---|
| A document identifying each individual important to the performance of the firm's CASS obligations (including the person with responsibility for CASS oversight) and the nature of their responsibility | CASS 10.2.1R(4) | Immediately |
| Any written notification or trust acknowledgement letters which must be given or received when a firm opens a client bank account or a client transaction account with a third party | CASS 10.2.1R(5) | Immediately |
| A copy of each agreement, side letter and/or amendment agreement with institutions where the firm deposits client money or safe custody assets | CASS 10.2.1R(5) | 48 hours |
| A document identifying and providing certain other information with respect to each group member and/or third party (a 'Third-Party Outsourcer') involved in the performance of operational aspects of the firm's obligations under CASS 6 or CASS 7 | CASS 10.2.1R(6) | 48 hours |
| A copy of each executed agreement, side letter and/or amendment agreement with any Third-Party Outsourcer | CASS 10.2.1R(7) | 48 hours |
| A document which describes how to (a) gain access to relevant information held by, and (b) effect a transfer of client money or safe custody assets held by, each Third-Party Outsourcer | CASS 10.2.1R(8) | 48 hours |
| A copy of the firm's manual in which are recorded its procedures for the management, recording and transfer of client money and safe custody assets | CASS 10.2.1R(9) | 48 hours |
| Records of the grounds upon which the firm satisfied itself of the appropriateness of its selection of each third-party with which it deposits safe custody assets | CASS 10.3.1R(1) | 48 hours |

| | | |
|---|---|---|
| In relation to clients the safe custody assets which have been used for securities financing transactions, records of (a) the consent from each such client to use the assets in question, and (b) the number of assets used | CASS 10.3.1R(2) | 48 hours |
| Records and accounts enabling the firm to distinguish safe custody assets of one client from those of another client or the firm's own assets | CASS 10.3.1R(3) | 48 hours |
| The most recent internal reconciliations relating to safe custody assets | CASS 10.3.1R(4A) | Immediately |
| A copy of every executed client agreement that includes a firm's right to use safe custody assets for its own account, including disclosure annexes from prime brokerage agreements | CASS 10.3.1R(4) | 48 hours |
| The most recent external reconciliations relating to safe custody assets | CASS 10.3.1R(4A) | Immediately |
| Records of the grounds upon which a firm satisfied itself as to the appropriateness of its selection of a third-party with which it has deposited client money | CASS 10.3.1R(6) | 48 hours |
| Records and accounts which enable the firm to distinguish the client money of one client from that of another client or the firm's own money | CASS 10.3.1R(7) | 48 hours |
| The most recent internal reconciliations relating to client money | CASS 10.3.1R(7A) | Immediately |
| The policy and procedures for carrying out custody record checks, custody reconciliations and client money reconciliations | CASS 10.3.1R(5A) | 48 hours |
| With respect to firms not using the 'standard method of internal client money reconciliation', written confirmation from the firm's auditor that the firm has adequate systems and controls in place | CASS 10.3.1R(5A) | 48 hours |

| The most recent external reconciliations relating to client money | CASS 10.3.1R(7A) | Immediately |
|---|---|---|
| A record of each client categorisation together with supporting documentation | CASS 10.3.1R(10) | 48 hours |
| A copy of any agreement pursuant to which a client is categorised or re-categorised | CASS 10.3.1R(10) | 48 hours |
| Copies of all client agreements with retail clients and professional clients | CASS 10.3.1R(11) | 48 hours |

## CASS 8 mandates

A mandate arises when a client gives authority to a CASS firm over their money or assets held with another separate firm. The mandate enables firms to give instructions in relation to the money or assets without the need for further client involvement.

Common examples of mandates include when firms look after assets held at a client's own custodian and fund managers who have authority over their client's bank account. However, the definition also includes direct debits, debit or credit card details recorded on phone calls and retained in a system.

Mandates are obtained by the firm from the client, and with the client's consent. They must be in written form at the time they are obtained from the client, and they must be retained by the firm.

A mandate enables a firm to give any or all of the types of instructions described below:

1. Instructions to another person in relation to the client's money that is credited to an account maintained by that other person for the client

2. Instructions to another person in relation to any money to which the client has an entitlement, where that other person is responsible to the client for that entitlement (including where that other person is holding client money for the client in accordance with CASS 5 or CASS 7)

3. Instructions to another person in relation to an asset of the client, where that other person is responsible to the client for holding that asset (including where that other person is safeguarding and administering investments, acting as trustee or depositary of an AIF or acting as trustee or depositary of a UCITS)

4. Instructions to another person such that the client incurs a debt or other liability to that other person or any other person (other than the firm); and

5. Their circumstances are such that the client's further involvement would not be necessary for the firm's instructions described in points 1-4 to be given effect.[8]

## Records and controls

When holding mandates, a firm must maintain adequate records and controls including:

- an up-to-date list of each mandate that the firm has obtained, including a record of any conditions placed by the client or the firm's management on the use of the mandate
- a record of each transaction entered into under each mandate
- internal controls to ensure that each transaction entered under a mandate is carried out in accordance with the mandate terms

---

[8] CASS 8.2.1

SECTION 4: REPORTING REQUIREMENTS

- details of the procedures and internal controls around the giving of instructions under mandates
- internal controls for the safeguarding of any passbook or similar document belonging to the client held by the firm (where the firm holds a client's passbook or similar documents).[9]

## CASS 9 – information to clients

CASS 9 generally deals with CASS 6 and 7 firms providing sufficient information to clients, however there are additional requirements for prime brokerage firms.

All CASS 6 and 7 firms must provide their clients with specific details about how the firm is holding their money and assets, and how certain arrangements might give rise to specific risks for those client's money or assets.

In addition, the rules require CASS 6 and 7 firms to send their clients a statement of the client money and assets holdings for that client at least once a year and whenever the client requests such a statement[10] (within 5 business days of receiving the request[11]).

## CASS 9 for prime brokers

Prime brokerage is the generic name for a bundled package of services offered by investment banks, wealth management firms, or securities dealers, to hedge funds which need the ability to borrow securities and cash in order to be able to invest on a netted basis and achieve an absolute return.

---

[9] CASS 8.3.2
[10] CASS 9.5.1
[11] CASS 9.5.5

A prime broker provides a centralised securities clearing facility for the hedge fund, so the hedge fund's collateral requirements are netted across all deals handled by the prime broker.

Prime brokerage services are provided by most of the largest financial services firms, including Goldman Sachs, UBS and Morgan Stanley.

CASS 9.2 requires prime brokerage firms to report to their clients on a daily basis on the total value of safe custody assets and total amount of client money as well as:

- The cash value of each of the following:
    - cash loans made to that client and accrued interest;
    - securities to be redelivered by that client under open short positions entered into on behalf of that client;
    - current settlement amount to be paid by that client under any futures contracts;
    - short sale cash proceeds held by the firm in respect of short positions entered into on behalf of that client;
    - cash margin held by the firm in respect of open futures contracts entered into on behalf of that client;
    - mark-to-market close-out exposure of any OTC transaction entered into on behalf of that client secured by safe custody assets or client money;
    - total secured obligations of that client against the prime brokerage firm; and
    - all other safe custody assets held for that client.
- Total collateral held by the firm in respect of secured transactions entered into under a prime brokerage agreement, including where the firm has exercised a

right of use in respect of that client's safe custody assets;
- The location of all a client's safe custody assets, including assets held with a sub-custodian; and
- A list of all the institutions at which the firm holds or may hold client money, including money held in client bank accounts and client transaction accounts.

The statement must be provided by the close of business of the next business day to the date of the statement.[12]

## Audit reporting

All regulated investment firms must send the FCA an annual CASS assurance report.[13] The annual CASS assurance report is completed by an external auditor, with the aim being to provide a reasonable assurance regarding the client money and/or custody assets held by the firm.

## Insolvency and Primary Pooling Events

Under the CASS rules, insolvency is referred to as a primary pooling event. The effectiveness of CASS compliance may only be evident in the event of an insolvency.

Once a firm fails, there is no recourse to the CASS rules. Firms who have kept to their CASS record-keeping requirements should be able to navigate insolvency in an orderly manner and promptly return client assets.

The common challenges are:

- Access to information systems

---

[12] CASS 9.2.1
[13] SUP 3.10.4

- Securing the return of client monies/assets
- Establishing individual client entitlements.

## Requirements under CASS 7A

From the time of the primary pooling event, CASS 7A.2.4R & CASS 7A.2.5R requires firms to:

- Calculate the client money entitlement for each affected client, applying any shortfall in the client money held to each of their entitlements.
- Make and retain a record of each client's share in the client money shortfall until each client is repaid.

This process must be completed for both general pools of client money and any sub-pools that have been created.

Any client money received after a primary pooling event should not be held with pre-existing client money. Instead, it should be placed in a client bank account opened after the primary pooling event.

## Sub-pools

A firm that is also a clearing member of an authorised central counterparty has the option of establishing legally and operationally separate sub-pools of client money. These are established for the benefit of a group of clients who have chosen to clear positions through a net margined omnibus client account maintained by the firm with that authorised central counterparty. [14]

---

[14] CASS 7.19.1

## SECTION 4: REPORTING REQUIREMENTS

The aim is to make it easier to resolve and pay out individual claims more quickly. The client money returned to some clients should also be maximised, as any client money shortfall would be restricted to beneficiaries of that sub-pool.

Each client money sub-pool requires its own client money bank and transaction accounts, with separate client money reconciliations and segregation being performed for each sub-pool[15] make them relatively expensive and complex to maintain.

### Secondary pooling event

Where a bank with whom client money is deposited fails to make good any shortfall (it may have to if liable e.g. it failed to exercise its duty of care) is known as a 'secondary pooling event'.

Requirements under CASS 7A:

1. From the time of the secondary pooling event, CASS 7A.3.8R requires firms to:

    a. Calculate a new client money entitlement for each affected client, applying any shortfall in the client money held by the deposit taker attributable to each of their entitlements.

    b. Make and retain a record of each client's share in the client money shortfall until each client is repaid.

2. There is no distinction between firms using one client money bank vs. firms using multiple client money bank accounts. Firms must calculate the exposure each client has to the bank that failed to determine the shortfall.

---

15 CASS 7.19.5

# SECTION 5:
# THE FCA

## FCA Approach

The FCA see CASS as a regulatory priority and maintains a specialist CASS supervision department.

The CASS supervision unit use the below methods to regulate CASS:

- Desk-based reviews
- CASS Audit reviews
- CMAR reviews
- Firm visits
- Ongoing relationship management (for large firms)
- Private warnings
- Fines.

## FCA Investigations and Actions

The key triggers for FCA investigations and actions are:

- Actual loss for clients
- Risk of loss to clients
- Failure to heed warnings from thematic work and final notices
- Lengthy breaches
- The size of the firm's CASS holdings
- Failure to identify breaches and notify the FCA
- False attestations
- Governance or cultural failings
- Previous fines.

## How to avoid or approach an FCA CASS investigation

To guard against an enforcement referral the firm should ensure:

- The firm has robust systems and controls that are reviewed on an ongoing basis
- The firm has an awareness of regulatory developments and actions
- The firm promptly notifies the FCA of any breaches
- The firm identifies and carries out remedial action on its own initiative.

To manage an FCA investigation effectively the firm should:

- Ensure prompt and well organised responses to requests for information and put forward well-prepared interviewees
- Put issues in context and show that actions were reasonable
- Seek to understand the FCA's concerns and address them early in the process
- Demonstrate the lack of risk to client assets
- Demonstrate the lessons learned and acted on by firm
- Settle if appropriate.

## Useful FCA contacts

For all CASS policy queries - **cassqueries@fca.org.uk**
For general queries - **cassgeneral@fca.org.uk**
For breach notifications - **cassriskinbox@fca.org.uk**

# SECTION 6:
# COMMON CASS FAILINGS

## Common CASS failings - identification

1. Not recognising what is and isn't a safe custody asset or client money.
2. Poor visibility over product features, contractual terms and obligations.
3. Lack of consideration given to intraday risk.
4. Ineffective management information.

## Common CASS failings - governance

1. Inadequate governance structure (reporting lines, terms of reference, CASS committee agenda items).
2. Lack of documented policies and procedure.
3. Lack of oversight and review of outsourced CASS processes.
4. Over-reliance on 'high level' assurance.
5. Lack of executive engagement with CASS with the CF10a or senior manager with responsibility for CASS operational oversight having insufficient influence.
6. Lack of CASS MI.

## Common CASS failings – scope of CASS

1. Failure to identify all instances of client assets arising in the business.
2. Failure to understand and control the inter-relationships with other group companies in respect of handling and protecting client assets.
3. Failure to consider matters on a product-by-product basis where client assets arise.

## Common CASS failings – reconciliations

1. Failure to ensure that reconciliations are complete and that the data used is accurate.
2. Failure to identify a non-standard approach to reconciliations.
3. Failure to ensure that the reconciliation method is in accordance with CASS rules.
4. Inadequate training for staff performing CASS reconciliations.

## Common CASS failings - segregation of client money

1. Failure to identify certain pots of client money that need client money protection.
2. Failure to ensure that segregation is effective i.e. inadequate, incomplete or missing trust letters.
3. Failure to fully understand the end to end life cycle of client money.
4. Failure to provide adequate guidance to staff on the importance of segregation and timely banking.

## Common CASS failings - segregation of custody assets

1. Failure to recognise the importance of custody assets protection.
2. Failure to undertake an "internal" custody assets reconciliation.
3. Failure to document a shortfall policy.
4. Failure to ensure that registration and l

## SECTION 6: COMMON CASS FAILINGS

**5.** Failure to ensure that 3rd party statements are retained.

## Common CASS failings - ineffective monitoring

**1.** Assumption that the firm can completely rely on the external audit of CASS.

**2.** Failure of internal audit and/or compliance to take a pro-active approach to CASS monitoring.

**3.** Failure of the compliance team to ensure that staff are adequately competent to undertake a CASS role and ensure that there is appropriate training.

## Common CASS failings - oversight of outsourced CASS functions

**1.** Where key CASS activities are outsourced firms fail to exercise appropriate oversight.

**2.** Failure to retain sufficient in-house CASS expertise to make any oversight effective.

**3.** Failure to keep appropriate evidence of effective oversight of outsourced CASS operations.

## Common CASS failings – breach reporting

**1.** Allowing breaches to recur without identifying or remediating the root cause.

**2.** Failure to properly document and record CASS breaches.

**3.** Unclear breach descriptions that do not allow firms to determine whether client assets were at risk.

**4.** Insufficient enquiries before providing notification to the FCA.

# SECTION 7:
# THE FUTURE OF CASS

## CASS Automation and Artificial Intelligence (AI)

The use of AI and automation has had a slow uptake thus far in CASS support functions, but it has the potential to be just as revolutionary as it has been in industries such as online media.

Many firms still rely on manual processes and spreadsheets to fulfil their CASS obligations, but this may be about to change. Any industry with repetitive tasks is ripe for automation and unfortunately many CASS tasks fit this description. As artificial intelligence begins to hit the front lines of CASS, it will be increasingly hard to justify spend on large CASS support headcount.

The good news is that AI and automation will eliminate the most mundane tasks associated within CASS compliance. Some firms are already moving away from manual spreadsheets to automated reconciliations, and this trend will continue. Some of the ancillary reconciliation tasks such as break investigations and breach reporting will also begin to be automated.

Some firms are also beginning to automate the CMAR, resolution pack and rule mapping processes. As these firms increase in number and size, the role of CASS support is likely to evolve in a review or supervisory role in the future.

However, it is likely that CASS specialists will still be needed to design and review any automated CASS systems and controls on an ongoing basis, to ensure that they meet requirements and continue to perform as expected.

# SECTION 8:
# WHY CASS REGULATION WILL BECOME BLOCKCHAIN REGULATION

## Introduction

Financial services are fundamentally based on keeping accurate records. These records could be the financial transactions, assets owned by the customers, amounts owed by the bank to its customers and the day-to-day operations.

Their accuracy is crucial to ensure that customers trust their financial institutions, market integrity is maintained, and customers are protected. This is why regulators require financial firms to comply with a variety of rules with regards to record keeping, including CASS.

The CASS rules help to keep client money separate from the firm's money and assets. If the firm fails and falls into receivership, the client money and assets can then be returned to the clients without becoming liable to creditor claims.

## What is blockchain

Blockchain is a type of distributed ledger technology (DLT) that forms the basis of bitcoin and other cryptocurrencies.

A simple way to understand blockchain is that it is a permanent ledger which records transactions. The transactions are bundled into blocks which point to other blocks and form a chain. Hence the name 'blockchain'.

The beauty about blockchains is that rather there being a single copy of these blocks, each node in the network maintains a copy of the blockchain, i.e. the complete ledger of transactions.

A node in the network is nothing but a server which runs a software corresponding to that blockchain and participates in the blockchain network.

If a new block of data is to be added to the blockchain, a majority of the nodes within the network, each of which possesses copies of the existing blockchain, must verify the proposed transaction.

All the transactions taking place in a network are added to blocks in the blockchain. If the block is verified by the network, then each node gets a copy of the block.

Blockchain also solves the problem of 'double spending' as the same asset can't be traded multiple times by a party to others.

## The purpose of CASS

CASS is a set of regulations passed by UK regulators to ensure the protection of client assets in case of insolvency of financial firms.

In particular:
CASS protects consumers' assets and money when a firm fails

- CASS enhances the integrity of the financial system by giving participants confidence that their money is protected upon insolvency; and
- the CASS rules set a minimum standard of protection that allows for a competitive market in investment and custodial services – not competing on levels of protection but on cost and the quality of services provided.

Financial Institutions must follow rules set out in the Client Assets Sourcebook (CASS) whenever they hold or control client money or safe custody assets as part of their business.

The collapse of Lehman Brothers in 2008, and MF Global, exposed failings in the FSA's client assets regime, as the clients of these firms didn't receive their money back in a timely fashion. This made the FSA rethink its client assets rules.

Consequently, a new chapter was inserted into CASS (which came into force in October 2012), requiring certain investment firms to have in place CASS Resolution Packs.

## Why is blockchain a superior method to CASS regulation?

The purpose of CASS regulation is to protect client assets and money when a firm fails. CASS enhances the integrity of the financial system by giving participants confidence that their money is protected upon insolvency.

As of now, regulators mostly rely on rule-based mechanisms to ensure client asset protection. CASS is an example of this, but blockchain technology provides a unique tool to solve these issues of regulation.

As discussed earlier, blockchains are immutable ledgers. Any transaction recorded on it is stored forever and can be audited at any later point of time. The nature of blockchain ensures that a single rogue admin or individual can't make any transactions without all nodes being able to see the transactions.

This is in sharp contrast to centralised databases and systems, where generally a single admin controls the database and there is a higher chance of fraud. Any transaction which is not in line with expectation can easily be tracked in a blockchain-based system and appropriate steps can be taken.

The inherent characteristics of blockchain technology make redundant a significant amount of regulatory architecture that would otherwise serve as a check on the risk of fraud or error.

For example, preventing the commingling of funds within a financial institution can now be achieved through the use of internal blockchains and automated technology. Smart contracts can be written on the underlying blockchain which can specify the rules to which the financial firms need to adhere to.

Even if a firm wishes to violate these rules, it is simply not possible, as the smart contract will not allow them. The rules will thus be codified and would be beyond human errors and frauds. The operation of the CASS rules, for instance, and its associated mechanisms in this environment have no meaning.

As an example, let's examine the use of blockchain for record-keeping in custody. The custody rules (CASS 6) are designed to restrict the mixing of client and the firm's assets and minimise the risk of the client's safe custody assets being used by the firm without the client's agreement. These rules also prevent client assets being treated as the firm's assets in the event of the firm's insolvency. These obligations require firms to maintain their records and accounts in a way to ensure their accuracy.

A blockchain based platform like Hyperledger can be used to create a decentralised ledger for this use case where the transactions done by the firm are recorded in the blockchain. The blockchain network can have nodes run by different parties including auditors and regulators. All transactions are executed through the smart contract, which ensures that the client money and assets are not used by the firm.

## Possible issues with the implementation of blockchain

While blockchain technology provides a disruptive way of enforcing regulation, it is still a new technology and comes with teething troubles.

Some possible issues could include implementation. Implementing blockchain mechanisms may not be straightforward for regulators and could pose many logistical and technical challenges.

Additionally, jurisdictional issues may pose a hurdle. For a cross-jurisdictional transaction, any node will come under the legislative umbrella of the location of the node. The blockchain would then need to be compliant with a potentially unwieldy number of legal and regulatory regimes.

## Conclusion

Blockchain is a foundational technology which will fundamentally change the way regulations in financial firms work. It is easy to see how CASS regulations could easily be made unnecessary by codifying the same rules using blockchain based technologies.

It's my belief that the rise of blockchain technology will eliminate the need for CASS regulations in the coming years.

# MY SERVICES

# MY SERVICES

I hope this book provides you with the necessary technical foundation to implement or review CASS systems and controls.

Some readers may desire a more tailored approach. Over the years I have become an expert in preventing firms and senior management from receiving multi-million pound fines from The FCA. I use my unique insight from FCA Enforcement cases and my experience as a CASS Supervisor to help my clients implement the necessary systems and controls to ensure compliance with the CASS rules and avoid significant fines. I have helped my clients implement CASS systems and controls of the highest standard.

I have set out my services below. Please do not hesitate to connect with me if you are interested in any of the below services or just say hello.

I am available at **asare.s.nicholls@visie.co.uk** or online at **www.visie.co.uk**

## Services:

- **Digital training:** I have put together specialist CASS training courses that are available online. Courses include CASS training for the Board, CASS training for CF10as and CASS managers, CASS training for staff and general CASS training for non-CASS staff.

- **In-person training:** I can also provide tailored classroom training for all purposes and all levels of staff depending on your requirements.

- **Internal audit and compliance monitoring review support:** I can provide CASS SME support for internal audit and compliance monitoring reviews of CASS at all stages including planning, testing and issue agreement.

- **Ongoing digital CASS support:** I can provide an ongoing CASS support service via instant messenger, email and phone to give expert CASS input at all levels via retainer.

- **CASS reviews:** I can provide targeted CASS reviews depending on your specific requirements. For example, I can review CASS reconciliations or custodian arrangements.

- **Secondments:** I can work at your firm on a secondment basis if you have specific role based or project needs.

- **Governance review and design:** I can help to review and design governance arrangements including committees, MI and oversight arrangements.

# BIBLIOGRAPHY

1. FCA Handbook
2. PS 14/9

# INDEX

## A

Accountability matrix  *26*
Acknowledgement Letters  *20, 35, 68, 69, 70, 112, 114*
Allocation of client money  *73*
Alternative approach  *13, 62, 63, 65, 66, 67, 89, 92*
Alternative approach record  *67*
Alternative approach to segregation  *13, 65*
Annual CASS assurance report  *42, 120*
Annual notification  *110*
Artificial Intelligence (AI)  *132*
Audit report. *Vedere* Annual CASS assurance report
Audit Reporting  *120*
Automation  *132*

## B

Banking exemption  *30, 50, 51, 73, 100*
Bare security interest  *58*
Behaviour that does not amount to market abuse  *16*
Blockchain  *133, 134, 135, 136, 137, 138*
Breaches  *17, 25, 28, 29, 31, 35, 37, 40, 41, 42, 43, 124, 125, 130*
Breach log  *26, 29*

## C

CASS 8  *16, 116, 117, 118*
CASS 9  *16, 103, 118, 119, 120*
CASS 10  *17, 111, 112, 113, 114, 115, 116*
CASS checklist  *26, 29*
CASS Firm type  *110*

CASS framework (CASS policy document) *26, 27*
CASS large *4, 12, 110*
CASS medium *110*
CASS Resolution Pack *17, 25, 26, 27, 36, 111, 112, 113, 136*
CASS small *110*
CASS universe *34, 35*
Central Counterparties (CCP) *64, 69, 70*
Cheques *79, 82, 93, 94, 95*
Cleared funds *37, 80*
Client agreements *26, 38, 61, 78, 103, 107, 112, 116*
Client categorisation *37, 54, 116*
Client Money *7, 9, 11, 12, 13, 14, 15, 16, 17, 20, 21, 25, 36, 38, 41, 48, 50, 51, 52, 53, 54, 56, 61, 62, 63, 64, 65, 66, 67, 68, 69, 70, 71, 72, 73, 74, 75, 76, 77, 78, 79, 80, 81, 82, 83, 84, 85, 86, 87, 89, 90, 91, 92, 93, 94, 95, 96, 100, 101, 102, 103, 104, 105, 106, 107, 108*
Client Money Held By Third Parties *72*
Client Money Relating To Custody Assets At Custodians *72*
Client Money Requirement *66, 67, 68, 89, 90, 91, 96*
Client Money Resource *68, 89, 96*
CMAR - Client Money And Asset Return *110*
COBS *19*
Collateral *16, 56, 57, 58, 95, 96, 100, 119*
Common CASS failings *128, 129, 130*
Compliance Monitoring *31, 33, 34, 141*
Custodian Agreement *71*
Custody Asset Registration *71*
Custody Reconciliations *96, 97, 98, 99, 115*

# D

De-minimis amounts *74*
Directions *16*
Discharge of fiduciary duty *61*
Discrepancies in Reconciliations *28, 40, 96, 98, 99, 100*
Diversification *28, 35, 105, 106*
Due diligence *27, 30, 36, 39, 40, 103, 104, 106*
DVP exemption *50, 52, 53, 54*

## E

EEA - European Economic Area  *49*
Eligible counterparties  *55, 56*
Evidential provision  *16*
Exemptions  *49, 50*
External custody reconciliations  *97, 98*

## F

FCA Approach  *124*
FCA Investigations & Actions  *124*
FCA visits  *29, 42*

## G

Governance  *7, 9, 21, 23, 24, 25, 27, 30, 35, 42, 44, 105, 124, 128, 141*
Guidance  *9, 16, 19, 36, 84, 129*

## H

House Account  *13, 64, 84, 86, 87, 88*

## I

Individual Client Balance Method Of Internal Client Money Reconciliation  *67, 68, 72, 89, 90, 91, 92, 94, 95, 96, 115*
Information to clients  *16, 118*
Insolvency. *Vedere* Primary Pooling Event
Interest  *10, 18, 19, 58, 77, 78, 79, 103, 119, 140*
Internal Audit  *9, 29, 31, 32, 33, 34, 130, 141*
Internal Client Money Reconciliation  *67, 68, 72, 89, 90, 91, 92, 96, 115*
Internal custody record checks  *96, 97*
Internal system evaluation method  *97*
Intra-Day Adjustments  *67*
Intraday Risk  *82, 128*
Intra-day Shortfall  *81, 82, 83*

## L

Liens  *72*

## M

Management Information  *24, 26, 28, 45, 128*
Mandates  *16, 36, 116, 117, 118*
Mandatory prudent segregation amount  *64, 66*
MiFID - The Markets in Financial Instruments Directive  *15, 19, 49*
Model A arrangement  *38*
Model B arrangement  *38*

## N

Net Negative Method Of Internal Client Money Reconciliation  *91, 92, 93*
Non-EEA  *49*
Non-Standard Method Of Internal Client Money Reconciliation  *91, 92*
Normal approach to segregation  *62*

## O

Outsourcing oversight  *39*

## P

Passporting  *49*
Permissions  *27, 48, 49, 53, 100*
Physical asset reconciliations  *96, 98*
Physical Receipts  *78*
Post transfer notifications  *108*
Pre-Funding  *82, 83, 84, 85, 86, 87, 88*
Primary pooling event  *13, 85, 120, 121*
Primary Pooling Events  *13, 120*
Prime Brokers  *56, 118*

Principle for Business *11, 16, 18, 40, 50, 81*
Procedures *25, 26, 28, 30, 31, 37, 53, 63, 75, 76, 80, 100, 101, 102, 103, 105, 112, 114, 115, 118*
Professional clients *55, 56, 74*
Prudent Segregation *36, 63, 64, 66, 79, 82, 83, 84, 85, 86, 87, 88, 93, 94, 95*
Prudent Segregation Record *85*

# R

RAO *19*
Rebates *78*
Reconciliation *13, 20, 26, 28, 30, 36, 37, 38, 40, 41, 44, 45, 52, 60, 67, 68, 72, 79, 88, 89, 90, 91, 92, 93, 94, 96, 97, 98, 99, 101, 102, 112, 115, 116, 122, 129, 132, 141*
Record keeping *17, 35, 134*
Rehypoyhecation *57*
Retail clients *55, 56, 57, 74, 77, 107, 116*
Reviews *21, 29, 31, 32, 33, 34, 124, 141*
Right to use *57, 58, 115*
Rules *8, 9, 11, 14, 15, 16, 17, 19, 26, 27, 30, 34, 38, 43, 44, 48, 49, 50, 51, 54, 56, 61, 63, 66, 67, 71, 75, 76, 77, 83, 84, 85, 88, 91, 92, 100, 108, 118, 120, 129, 134, 135, 136, 137, 138, 140*
Rules map *26, 27*

# S

Secondary Pooling Event *122*
Segregation *13, 20, 36, 45, 60, 62, 63, 64, 65, 66, 79, 82, 83, 84, 85, 86, 87, 88, 89, 91, 92, 93, 94, 95, 122, 129*
Settlement *36, 50, 52, 53, 63, 80, 81, 82, 119*
Shortfalls in custody reconciliations *99, 100, 101*
Statements of principle for approved persons *16*
Sub-Pools *121*
SYSC *19, 39*

# T

Temporary handling of custody assets  50
The Board  25, 30, 141
The FCA  4, 7, 9, 11, 12, 14, 15, 16, 17, 18, 19, 20, 21, 29, 32, 33, 39, 41, 42, 43, 44, 48, 49, 65, 79, 81, 83, 84, 86, 102, 103, 107, 110, 111, 112, 113, 120, 123, 124, 125, 130, 140
Third Party Administrator (TPA)  38, 39
Three lines of defence  27, 30, 31, 32
Title Transfer Collateral Arrangements  56, 100
Training  10, 21, 25, 26, 29, 30, 35, 37, 38, 105, 129, 130, 141
Transfer of business  61, 106, 108
Trust Law  19, 20

# U

Unbreakable Term Deposits  77
Unclaimed Client Money  61, 74, 75, 76, 77
Unclaimed Custody Assets  74, 75, 76, 103

Printed in Great Britain
by Amazon